The Adaptable Country

Canadian Essentials

Series editor: Daniel Béland

Provocative thinking and accessible writing are more necessary than ever to illuminate Canadian society and to understand the opportunities and challenges that Canada faces. A joint venture between McGill-Queen's University Press and the McGill Institute for the Study of Canada, this series arms politically active readers with the understanding necessary for engaging in – and improving – public debate on the fundamental issues that have shaped our nation. Offering diverse and multidisciplinary perspectives on the leading subjects Canadians care about, Canadian Essentials seeks to make foundational and cutting-edge knowledge more accessible to informed citizens, practitioners, and students. Each title in this series aims to bolster individual action in order to support a better, more inclusive and dynamic country. Canadian Essentials welcomes proposals for concise and well-written books dealing with far-reaching and timely Canadian topics from a broad swath of authors, both within and outside of academia.

1 COVID-19
A History
Jacalyn Duffin

2 Canada and Climate Change
William Leiss

3 The Adaptable Country
How Canada Can Survive the Twenty-First Century
Alasdair Roberts

The Adaptable Country

How Canada Can Survive the Twenty-First Century

Alasdair Roberts

McGill-Queen's University Press
Montreal & Kingston • London • Chicago

ISBN 978-0-2280-2200-8 (paper)
ISBN 978-0-2280-2201-5 (ePDF)
ISBN 978-0-2280-2202-2 (ePUB)

Legal deposit third quarter 2024
Bibliothèque nationale du Québec

Printed in Canada on acid-free paper that is 100% ancient forest free (100% post-consumer recycled), processed chlorine free

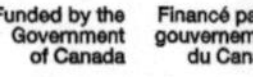

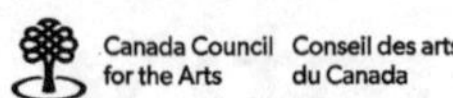

We acknowledge the support of the Canada Council for the Arts.
Nous remercions le Conseil des arts du Canada de son soutien.

McGill-Queen's University Press in Montreal is on land which long served as a site of meeting and exchange amongst Indigenous Peoples, including the Haudenosaunee and Anishinabeg nations. In Kingston it is situated on the territory of the Haudenosaunee and Anishinaabek. We acknowledge and thank the diverse Indigenous Peoples whose footsteps have marked these territories on which peoples of the world now gather.

LIBRARY AND ARCHIVES CANADA CATALOGUING IN PUBLICATION

Title: The adaptable country : how Canada can survive the twenty-first century / Alasdair Roberts.
Names: Roberts, Alasdair (Alasdair Scott), author.
Series: Canadian essentials ; 3.
Description: Series statement: Canadian essentials ; 3 | Includes bibliographical references and index.
Identifiers: Canadiana (print) 20240375114 | Canadiana (ebook) 20240375173 | ISBN 9780228022008 (paper) | ISBN 9780228022022 (ePUB) | ISBN 9780228022015 (ePDF)
Subjects: LCSH: Canada—Politics and government—21st century—Forecasting. | LCSH: Canada—Social conditions—21st century—Forecasting. | LCSH: Canada—Economic conditions—21st century—Forecasting.
Classification: LCC JL65 .R63 2024 | DDC 320.971—dc23

Contents

Preface

In a 2022 survey conducted by Leger Marketing, almost 70 per cent of Canadians between the ages of fifteen and forty said they anticipated major upheavals – events like war, mass population movements, and natural disasters – in the foreseeable future. Almost 60 per cent believed that Canadian governments were not doing anything about these dangers and that governments were betraying young Canadians by their failure to prepare for the challenges of their time. The same proportion of respondents said that they felt helpless in the face of society's problems. "Young Canadians express real fears about the future," the study concluded. "They do not trust traditional institutions to make things better."

The young Canadians who expressed these views are not mistaken. The remaining decades of this century will be very difficult. The country will face major upheavals. And Canadian governments are not doing all they could to prepare for these challenges.

This book explains why. It starts with the premise that political systems must be adaptable if they are to survive and thrive. An adaptable system is one that is capable of anticipating long-term challenges, generating an effective grand strategy for meeting the whole set of anticipated challenges, building support for that strategy, and translating that strategy into action. Adaptability is especially important in periods of extreme turbulence, like the epoch we are entering now.

The adaptability of the Canadian political system cannot be taken for granted. The system is designed on the principle that political power should be widely diffused and individual freedom should be respected. This design promotes adaptability in some ways but threatens it in others. At its worst, the system may be vulnerable to short-sightedness, confusion, and gridlock. Policy-makers in Canada should always think carefully about how to maximize the system's strengths and minimize its vulnerabilities.

My argument is that policy-makers are not doing this sort of thinking as much as they ought to, or even as much as they used to. In several ways, the country's capacity to formulate and execute grand strategy has declined. This is a serious but remediable problem. In the final chapter, I suggest reforms that would improve adaptability within the system as a whole.

I developed the argument in this book while serving as the Jocelyne Bourgon Visiting Scholar at the Canada School for Public Service in 2022–23. It expands on the lecture that I delivered at the school in July 2023. The book itself is based entirely on evidence drawn from publicly available sources. I was also guided by interviews with almost one hundred people inside and outside government, with experience spanning almost sixty years.

My argument is neither exhaustive nor definitive. Every part could have been explored in more depth, and there are important topics that I have omitted. For example, time constraints prevented me from examining the capabilities of provincial, territorial, municipal, and Indigenous governments. A more complete assessment of adaptability would include these important components of the Canadian political system.

Here are some ways in which my argument could be misguided. I may overestimate the fragility of states in general. I might be wrong in thinking that adaptability is the key to state survival, and I might be wrong in my enumeration of the systemic functions essential to adaptability. While looking specifically at Canada, I may have focused on the wrong parts of the system, emphasizing some too much while neglecting others. And I might simply be wrong in my diagnosis of one part or another.

While reading this book, it is important to distinguish between these types of error. Readers might conclude that I have focused on the wrong parts of the Canadian political system or that my assessment of those parts is mistaken. Obviously, I hope that this is not the case, but even if it is, I encourage readers to step back and think about the bigger questions. Do we agree about the magnitude of the dangers facing the country? Do we agree that, in general, adaptability is an essential quality for political systems, and about my definition of what adaptability requires? And if we agree on the dangers, and the importance of adaptability in general, where else in the Canadian system should we look for vulnerabilities?

These are urgent questions. The well-being of Canadians in coming decades depends on the capacity of the political system to anticipate and manage a profusion of hazards competently. There is a larger challenge too. There are many people who doubt the capacity of open societies like Canada to navigate through turbulent times. Skepticism about the adaptability of democratic systems might explain the recent slide toward authoritarianism around the world. Even in the West, some experts argue that authoritarian systems do a better job of protecting people in periods of extreme stress. Our assignment in this century is to make the case for freedom: that is, to show how systems designed to respect diversity and human rights can also respond nimbly to existential threats.

The Adaptable Country

1

Adaptability and Why It Matters

No political system lasts forever. Some systems expire after only a few decades; a handful last for centuries. A system might plunge into crisis and emerge in a different form, still governing roughly the same territory. Or it might fracture into many smaller systems. Or it might be absorbed into a larger system. One way or another, though, every system ends eventually. Leaders rarely acknowledge this fact – for understandable reasons – but it is a hard reality.

In the 1970s, Estonian political scientist Rein Taagepera calculated the lifespan of empires throughout history. Before World War II, most people lived within empires. Empires were the default mode of political organization, but they were also mortal. Taagepera calculated that the average duration of empires throughout history was three or four generations. Most were short-lived. Fewer than one-fifth of the empires in Taagepera's study lasted for more than ten generations.

After World War II, the remaining empires were broken up, and states became the default mode of political organization. A state is a political system that exercises control over a defined territory and is recognized as the legitimate authority in that territory by other states. There are roughly 190 states in the world today, and Canada is one of them.

We take the world of states for granted, but it is just as brittle as the world of empires. Most states are very young. Two-thirds of the states represented in the United Nations General Assembly are less than eighty years old. Most states are also unstable, according to the research organization Fund for Peace. About half the world's population lives in *very* unstable states. Several states have collapsed within the life experience of the average Canadian, which is about forty-three years. The most striking example of state collapse in recent decades is that of the Soviet Union in 1991.

We can list the problems that have contributed to the collapse of political systems in the past. The list includes rebellions by regional leaders, popular uprisings, invasions, economic shocks, plagues, mass migrations, and climate change among other disruptions. However, a political system rarely collapses for just one reason. Usually, collapse happens because problems pile up. One problem aggravates another, which aggravates yet another. Political leaders and government agencies are overwhelmed. The entire situation becomes too complex to understand and manage, and the system unravels. This dire scenario is called a polycrisis.

The structure of any state, including Canada, can be seen as an apparatus for avoiding, or at least managing, problems that are potentially fatal to that state and, above all, for avoiding a polycrisis. For example, we give substantial power to provinces to reduce the risk of regional rebellions. We give people the right to vote to reduce the risk of mass discontent. We establish an army to protect against invasion, police forces to reduce internal disorder, regulatory agencies to prevent economic collapse, a public health system to avoid pandemics, and so on. In a sense, the state as a whole is like a giant risk management scheme.

Of course, we have positive goals for the state as well. We want to build a just and prosperous society, but this is only possible if the state itself survives. Political leaders must anticipate the worst case, so that they can work toward the best case. Leaders must be vigilant about potential dangers. They must devise a grand strategy for achieving their ambitions, given the dangers they are likely to face. They must generate agreement about the wisdom of their proposed strategy. And they must build or renovate governmental institutions so that they are capable of doing all that the strategy requires.

Moreover, leaders must be prepared to revise their work. The world is a complicated place. Some threats abate with time while new ones come into view. Think about all the dangers Western countries have encountered so far this century that were dismissed as unimportant in the year 2000: terrorism, financial crises, pandemics, gross inequality, ethno-nationalism, and war. For any state, the threat matrix, as security specialists call it, is constantly evolving. In a world like this, vigilance can never be relaxed. Grand strategy always requires readjustment. Institutions must be renovated constantly to meet the new requirements of strategy.

THE REALIST PERSPECTIVE

The view of governance I have just described is known as realism. It emphasizes the prevalence of danger, the fragility of states, the need for vigilance, and the importance of nimbleness in adjusting strategy and institutions to accommodate new circumstances.

In the Western world, one of the most famous advocates of realism in governance is Niccolò Machiavelli. Today, Machiavelli has a reputation for encouraging dirty politics. This is unfair to Machiavelli and, for present purposes, beside the point. We are interested in Machiavelli's broader view of what governing a state requires.

In two of his most famous books, *The Prince* and *The Discourses*, Machiavelli describes a world that is confused and fraught with perils. Political leaders wrestle with shifting circumstances, which Machiavelli calls Fortune and compares to "one of those violent torrents that flood the plains, destroying trees and buildings, hurling earth from one place to another." The best way to deal with Fortune, Machiavelli says, is by building "dikes and dams in times of calm, so that when the torrent rises it will gush into a channel, its force neither so harmful nor so unbridled."

A good political system, in Machiavelli's view, is ready to bear foreseeable hazards. But the set of potential hazards varies by place and time. "All the affairs of this world are in motion," he warns. "Fortune is changeable." A leader must watch carefully for new threats and build new dikes and dams – new institutions – where necessary. Renovating institutions is hard but essential work. "States that have a long life," Machiavelli concludes, "are those which can keep renewing themselves. It is quite clear that if they do not renew themselves they will not endure."

Machiavelli did not invent realism. He was one of dozens of scholars who wrote handbooks for rulers around the world in the centuries before the Enlightenment. Look at the work of Kautilya, a celebrated thinker in Indian political philosophy. His *Arthashastra*, written two millennia ago, is obsessed with the ephemerality of political order. Kautilya details all the calamities that might befall the Mauryan empire, which ruled much of the Indian subcontinent around the third century BCE. Survival, Kautilya warns Mauryan leaders, requires foresight, preparedness, and quick adjustment to changing conditions.

Realism pervades the millennia-long history of Chinese statecraft. "Everything on earth is subject to change," says an ancient text, the *I Ching*. "Evil can be held in check but not permanently abolished." It follows that a good leader must "be mindful of danger in times of peace, downfall in times of survival, and chaos in times of stability." A seasoned observer of China attributes the country's endurance over centuries to its "seemingly unlimited capacity for metamorphosis and adaptation" and refusal to be "trapped into set forms."

We can see elements of realism in the political thinking and practices of America's Indigenous peoples. Pre-colonial Indigenous societies, says Roxanne Dunbar-Ortiz, "were dynamic social systems with adaptation built into them." White colonization was a calamity for these societies. Survival required agility in the face of centuries of oppression. In a recent book, Pekka Hämäläinen charts the history of the Lakota people, who have endured, he argues, because of their "stunning ability and willingness to change" while preserving the essence of Lakota identity. The "shapeshifting Lakota regime," as Hämäläinen calls it, takes inspiration from Iktómi, the spider-trickster, who can transform himself at will into any form.

The early twentieth century saw a revival of the realist perspective among the settler populations of North America. American and Canadian intellectuals recognized that public institutions built in the eighteenth and nineteenth centuries were no longer suited to societies convulsed by economic, technological, and cultural change. In 1927, American philosopher John Dewey said government ought to be regarded as a never-ending "experimental process." A professor at the University of Toronto, Robert MacIver, agreed. "The state," he said, "never achieves a final perfected form. It is a domain of constant innovation."

Realist thinking thrives whenever societies enter moments of severe stress. Writing in 1973, during another period of social and economic disorder in the United States, Professor Donald Schön said it was time to abandon belief in the "stable state." The truth, said Schön, was that no set of governing institutions was likely to remain workable for more than a few decades. The task for policy-makers was to guide a never-ending process of institutional transformation. In 2016, another moment of deep stress in the United States, Schön's message was echoed by Professor Donald Kettl: "The challenge of adapting government to shifting problems is ageless and universal." He added that "the biggest challenge of governance, across the globe, is adapting the institutions and processes of government to the new problems it faces."

ANTI-REALISM

Not everyone is a realist. Throughout history, there have been philosophers and politicians who have emphasized the need for continuity in the design of political systems rather than change. These anti-realists come in different varieties.

One kind of anti-realist is the hardline constitutionalist. The premise of hardline constitutionalism is that we know enough about the world to set up a scheme of government that will work for a very long time. The operating rules for this political system can be spelled out in detail in a constitution, a foundational document that is hard to change.

By contrast, realists are skeptical about constitutions that are highly detailed and inflexible, precisely because realists anticipate the need to adjust and reinvent institutions as conditions change.

The American constitution was drafted by hardline constitutionalists. According to a famous nineteenth-century jurist, it was "reared for immortality." President Woodrow Wilson said it was designed on "the Newtonian theory of the universe." He meant that drafters of the constitution saw the political world as though it were a piece of clockwork, composed of well-defined pieces interacting in predictable ways. "Study government," said one of the drafters, John Adams, "as you construct steam engines." Today, the tradition of hardline constitutionalism is continued by legal scholars who insist the American constitution must be interpreted exactly as it would have been in the eighteenth century.

Hardline constitutionalism does not have deep roots in Canada. Still, political leaders have expressed an appreciation for it now and then. In 1987, Pierre Trudeau said the recently modified Canadian constitution had established a system of government that would "last a thousand years." This was an unusual sort of comment for Trudeau, who would normally be classed as a realist. Trudeau was frustrated with politicians who wanted to revise the constitution he had worked so hard to bring home to Canada in 1982. Some of those politicians might have been affected by anti-realist thinking too. They thought the 1982 constitution was flawed but that, properly amended, it would "finally resolve" problems that threatened to tear the country apart.

A second kind of anti-realism can be found in the political theory known as neo-liberalism. Neo-liberalism is a political philosophy that emerged after World War II and became influential around the world by the end of the twentieth century. A central tenet of neo-liberalism is that elected politicians have strong incentives to make decisions that damage long-term growth. The authority of politicians has to be curtailed, for the good of the country.

As Thomas Friedman famously said in 1999, neo-liberals want politicians to don a "golden straitjacket." The straitjacket includes strict rules against borrowing money that would ideally be entrenched in a national constitution. Central banks must be given iron-clad independence, so they can fight inflation without interference. International agreements, enforced by bodies such as the World Trade Organization, must be established to stop governments from interfering with trade and investment across national borders. There are other elements to the straitjacket too.

Arrangements like these are sometimes called commitment devices, because they commit decisionmakers to policies that make sense in the long run but are politically awkward in the short run. Politicians surrender their freedom to avoid mistakes, just as Odysseus tied himself to the mast so that he would not be lured onto the rocks by the Sirens.

Organizations like the International Monetary Fund and the World Bank played a significant role in spreading such reforms around the world in the last years of the twentieth century. The list of reforms that they recommended is widely known as the Washington Consensus. It was regarded as a universal formula for governance, good for all times and places.

No realist would ever talk about a universal formula for governing well. A realist would say every state must find its own way as history unfolds. But in the 1990s powerful people believed that the world had reached "the end of history," a new plateau of stability in which most of the fundamental problems confronting states had been resolved. The world would witness the emergence of the "final form of human government," that system of market-friendly democracy prescribed by the Washington Consensus. Even communist China seemed to be following a path toward economic and political liberalization.

Of course, history was rebooted in the twenty-first century, as one crisis followed another. One result was that the Washington Consensus, the universal formula for governing well, was consigned to the dustbin. Institutional reforms of the 1990s were not abandoned, but they were challenged everywhere. Borrowing limits were ignored, central bank independence was infringed, trade rules were bent, and governments intervened more directly in their economies. Governments improvised as they reacted to one shock after another. Politicians were realists again.

DEFINING ADAPTABILITY

At a very high level of abstraction, leaders in every state have similar goals. They generally want security from external threats, internal order, prosperity, and some conception (perhaps quite different from ours) of a just society. However, these are all vague concepts, and leaders must refine what they mean in practice across differing circumstances. Additionally, these goals often conflict with one another, so leaders must decide which ones rank higher. Leaders must also decide what broad lines of policy are most effective for achieving these goals.

The bundle of ideas about priorities and policies that eventually emerges constitutes a grand strategy. Academics also refer to this bundle of ideas as a governing paradigm or a ruling ideology.

It may be hard to believe, in this age of polarization, that a large and diverse country such as Canada could have a coherent and generally accepted grand strategy. But, think about the fundamentals that almost all Canadians take for granted: liberal democracy, market capitalism, federalism, a welfare state, and so on. Canadians argue about what these concepts mean in practice, but who would abandon any one of them entirely? These are elements of a grand strategy for governing Canada that has evolved over decades. The state apparatus – the complex of institutions that make up the Canadian system of government – has been constructed to fit this grand strategy. Think of grand strategy as an architect's plan for a house and the state apparatus as the house itself.

Realists believe there is no perfect strategy that works at all times and in all places. Our ideas about security, order, prosperity, and social justice evolve over time. For example, Prime Minister Pierre Trudeau's "just society" of 1968 seems unjust in many ways today. Among other changes, Canadians have more enlightened ideas about 2SLGBTQI+ and Indigenous rights. New circumstances – terror attacks, protests, economic slumps, wildfires – also cause us to readjust our priorities. Experience makes us question the wisdom of old policies, while observation of other countries makes us curious about new ones. For these reasons, leaders and citizens will revise their overall strategy for governing the country.

A change in strategy must be followed by renovation of the state apparatus. Old institutions are demolished or renovated, and new ones are built, to put the renovated strategy into practice. As any homeowner knows, renovation is not easy. Left to the last minute, and done without some degree of planning, it turns out badly. So far as possible, renovation should be done deliberately and thoughtfully.

Adaptability refers to the ability of a country to renovate its grand strategy and institutions in response to new circumstances and ideas. Any country that hopes to survive and thrive for more than a few decades must be adaptable in this way. Countries that cannot alter their strategy and institutions will fall prey to foreign influences, suffer from secessionism and internal unrest, stagnate economically, and become increasingly unjust. In the worst case, they will collapse entirely.

The Soviet Union is one example of a country that suffered this fate. Its last leader Mikhail Gorbachev recognized that his country needed a new grand strategy and established a process for finding one. Gorbachev called this process *perestroika*, which means restructuring. He wanted to forestall economic and social collapse through "renewal of every aspect of Soviet life." The effort was too little, too late. The Soviet state was too brittle to change course, and it ceased to exist in 1991.

Adaptability is not the same as crisis management. Crises arise when societies confront grave challenges for which they are not prepared. Certainly, governments should manage crises effectively, but we would prefer that crises not arise at all. In general, crises arise when a governing strategy has fallen out of sync with changing circumstances. Old institutions are unprepared for new threats. Crises are often preceded by a long period in which portents of danger are ignored by political leaders. The eventual crisis is evidence of a failure to anticipate danger or, in other words, a failure to adapt.

Similarly, adaptability is not the same as resilience. Resilience has been defined as "the capacity of a system to preserve its core purpose and integrity in the face of dramatically changed circumstances." In the short run, of course, resilience is desirable. Any political system must have the ability to survive sudden shocks. However, the trauma of this experience might make people reconsider the purpose of the system. People may want to devise a new system rather than simply preserving the status quo. For example, Canada has not merely weathered shocks over the last forty years. These shocks have pushed the country to redefine its priorities. Among other important changes, it has become more open and inclusive. This higher-level rethinking of goals is an important component of adaptability.

FOUR ESSENTIAL FUNCTIONS

We should be able to look at the design of a political system and judge whether that design promotes or obstructs adaptability. We want to look at not only formal institutions – the rules of the game that dictate how power will be distributed and exercised – but also the informal practices embedded in the daily routines of governing. Additionally, we want to look at the role of organizations that are not strictly part of the governmental apparatus, such as political parties, the media, interest groups, think tanks, universities, and social movements. We are interested in political culture too: that is, the bundle of ideas that guide our thinking about the aims and methods of politics.

When we look at the political system, defined in this broad way, we should ask four questions.

1 *Is the system capable of anticipating dangers?* We want people who exercise power, or who influence those power-holders, to be looking down the road for hazards. In other words, we want them to be vigilant. At a fundamental level, this means leaders must be aware that there are hazards. They should not be distracted by immediate problems or blinded by hubris. Leaders also need organizational support to engage in forward-thinking. Somewhere in the system there should be people with the skills and resources to help leaders identify risks and gauge their importance.

2 *Can the system redesign strategy to address long-term challenges?* Identifying long-term dangers is not enough. The system must be capable of imagining how public and private institutions could be reconfigured to manage those dangers. Technocrats usually talk about defining "policy options" for meeting new problems, but this understates the magnitude of the task. Major challenges are always intertwined, and they must be addressed comprehensively. We are talking about a substantial reconfiguration of an approach to governance, about the invention of a new grand strategy, including a plan for overhauling institutions in line with this strategy. Again, think of this as making plans for a home renovation. For any substantial renovation, you need an architect and blueprints.

3 *Is the system capable of building political support for the proposed strategy?* Suppose far-sighted leaders have recognized dangers on the horizon and formulated a clever plan for addressing them. To put this newly crafted governing strategy into action, one more hurdle must be overcome. Powerful constituencies must be persuaded that the new strategy is sound. When faced with unwilling groups, the only alternative to persuasion available to leaders is imposing a new strategy by force. However, there are practical and moral limits to the use of force. Even in authoritarian systems, leaders must present a plausible case to powerful stakeholders and the general public that a proposed course of action makes sense. Any system must be capable of legitimation, the process of building the political support necessary to execute a proposed change in strategy.

4 *Is the system capable of executing a proposed strategy – that is, of renovating institutions and mobilizing resources as the strategy requires?* The line between legitimation and execution can be blurry. Obviously, putting a new strategy in place requires the support or acquiescence of politically powerful groups.

However, it also involves very practical work, such as dismantling old bureaucracies and building new ones, drafting and enforcing new laws, imposing taxes and spending money. We can imagine a system in which stakeholders are generally agreed about goals but incapable of achieving those goals in practice. A well-designed strategy could be mangled by incompetent or uncooperative civil servants, or by public agencies that refuse to coordinate.

In sum, we have identified four functions that are essential for adaptability in any political system. As shorthand, call these four functions: anticipation, redesign, legitimation, and execution. When we look at any governmental system, we should ask whether its institutions, practices, and culture enable it to perform these four functions well.

CAN FEDERAL-LIBERAL-DEMOCRATIC SYSTEMS PERFORM THESE FUNCTIONS?

In everyday conversation, "the system" is sometimes interpreted as a combination of institutions that are tightly integrated and think and work in a coordinated way. In this view, a system is almost like a person who sets a goal and pursues it rationally. We can see how such a system might be capable of formulating a grand strategy, maybe even putting it in writing, and then making all the institutional adjustments required to execute it. We imagine highly centralized, authoritarian systems like China might work this way.

Obviously, Canada is not an authoritarian system. On the contrary, the country's political system is typified by the broad diffusion of power. The system is *federal* because authority is formally divided between levels of government, with independent courts protecting the authority of each level. The system is *liberal* because it recognizes a sphere of individual freedom, defined in the language of rights, which is also protected by courts. The system is *democratic* because public opinion, expressed through elections and other channels, decides who will occupy the most critical positions in government and the main characteristics of government policy.

For convenience, I will call this a federal-liberal-democratic (FLD) system of government. People sometimes talk about "Western democracies," but the terms are not equivalent, as not all Western democracies are federations.

In FLD systems, no one person is completely in charge. Prime ministers can declare national priorities, but many other actors – premiers, legislators, voters, judges, and others – cannot be fully bound by that declaration or bound at all. Similarly, prime ministers can propose new policies, but other actors can refuse to implement them. Even within the federal government, a prime minister's ability to accomplish goals may be sharply limited.

It may be difficult to see how such a system would be capable of performing the four functions that are essential to adaptability. Who exactly anticipates dangers and formulates grand strategy? Indeed, does it even make sense to talk about grand strategy in this context? Who does the pulling and hauling necessary to build political agreement, and who ensures that agencies located at different levels of government act in a coordinated way?

Defenders of the FLD model, including philosophers such as John Dewey and Karl Popper, argue that it is capable of performing the four functions essential to adaptability. In fact, they claim FLD systems perform better than authoritarian regimes precisely because power is so broadly distributed. According to these defenders, we should not look for any one institution within the system that bears primary responsibility for executing any of these four functions. The virtue of an FLD system, they say, is that *everyone* is responsible, to some degree, for these functions. An FLD system is like a network of computers rather than a single mainframe. The system distributes responsibility widely and, as a result, harnesses more analytic power. The system also has the advantage of redundancy: if one part fails, another picks up the slack. Every component is backed up and every proposed action is error tested.

To put the argument more concretely, the Achilles heel of any authoritarian system is its dependence on the centre. If the top leadership is not monitoring for hazards or lacks competence in crafting strategy, then the results are fatal for the entire system. In an FLD system, a much wider range of groups and individuals are empowered to warn about looming dangers. Freedom of thought and expression allow for more creativity throughout society in devising responses to those dangers. Lower-level governments can act like laboratories, experimenting with alternative responses to new problems.

Authoritarian systems rely heavily on propaganda and repression as instruments to build political support for, or at least quash resistance to, shifts in national strategy. Proponents of FLD systems argue that propaganda and repression are clumsy instruments for overcoming opposition to new policies. The virtue of open debate and free elections is that these processes generate deeper public understanding of the reasons for shifts in national strategies. As a result, political support is more robust. Free elections are also an efficient way of removing inattentive or incompetent leaders.

In an FLD system, grand strategy is the eventual result of all of this argument and negotiation. For this reason, some scholars say the strategy is emergent rather than calculated. The strategy is not suddenly revealed. It is not formally stated in any single document. It is not the property of one party or agency. Rather, grand strategy is manifested in understandings about national priorities and policies that are widely shared by political leaders, bureaucrats, voters, and interest groups. These understandings are the product of dialogue and bargaining. Obviously, there is never unanimity on all aspects of grand strategy. At a certain point, disagreement on some policy might be so deep that it would be unreasonable to describe it as part of a country's grand strategy.

However, when grand strategy does exist, it binds an FLD system together. This is what defenders of the model argue. Governments and citizens may have formal autonomy, but they are more likely to move in the same direction because they understand the overall strategy. Or, at the very least, collisions are minimized because areas of disagreement are clearly designated. In any case, the risks of miscoordination are reduced, and policies are more likely to be executed properly.

Defenders of the FLD model make one final argument. Leaders in authoritarian systems are limited in their ability to oversee the large bureaucracies that are necessary to execute national policies. There is only so much that they can see and control. As a result, authoritarian bureaucracies are often sluggish, wasteful, and corrupt. In FLD systems, however, bureaucracies are exposed to public scrutiny, making it more likely that such problems will be identified and corrected. Bureaucracies in FLD systems might be split between different levels of government, making coordination more challenging, but this disadvantage is offset by the fact that each level of bureaucracy is more effective.

Much of this argument for why FLD systems are adaptable is accepted as common sense in the West. However, the case is not open-and-shut. It hinges on contestable assumptions about culture, institutions, and practices within FLD systems.

In terms of culture, advocates of the FLD model are children of the Enlightenment. They assume people are concerned about the future, good at reasoning about complicated problems, and willing to engage in civil debate. Yet skeptics question whether democratic culture has lived up to Enlightenment ideals. Starting in the 1960s, critics began to complain about the emergence of consumer societies in which people spent more time chasing fashion than they did planning for the future. They argued that in good times, people indulge in luxuries rather than preparing for a rainy day. In bad times, they betray future generations by running up the government debt. Or people destroy the environment for the sake of immediate economic gains.

Other skeptics have wondered about the rationality of citizens in democratic systems. Research shows that voters often overestimate their own knowledge, block out inconvenient information, and dismiss the advice of experts. Sometimes, voters simply refuse to do the hard work of thinking carefully. People are prone to hubris during periods of prosperity, thinking that they have mastered the world's problems. In 1996, an American policy-maker called this "irrational exuberance." When things are going poorly, however, the popular mood swings in the opposite direction. In these moments, citizens are prone to despair, thinking that nothing can be done to prevent social and economic collapse.

Another perceived weakness, from the point of view of culture, is the refusal of some citizens to resolve their differences amicably. Friedrich Nietzsche said in the nineteenth century that men had a "thirst for enemies," and in the late twentieth century, many political psychologists agreed. Internal divisions within FLD systems seem to deepen in moments of stress, just when social and political co-operation is most important. Complaints about the decline of civility in Western democracies mounted after the global financial crisis of 2007–08. Today, some voters are consumed by paranoid theories about the power of opposing groups.

The vulnerabilities of FLD systems may be institutional as well as cultural. For example, economists in the 1970s began worrying that elections encourage politicians to fixate on the short term rather than the long term. Politicians spend extravagantly to buy the support of voters, refuse to eliminate obsolete programs, decline to take painful steps to curb inflation, and neglect public investments that will only pay off in the distant future. Many neo-liberal reforms of the late twentieth century, elements of the "golden straitjacket," were intended to correct the perceived short-term bias of electoral politics.

Another signature feature of the FLD model – the division of governmental powers between executive, legislative, and judicial branches of government – may also threaten adaptability. The separation of powers protects freedom, improves government accountability, and creates space for public debate. However, critics in the late twentieth century began to raise concerns that the separation of powers could also be debilitating. Divided authority delays action and sometimes prevents it entirely. It also creates more openings for special interests to apply pressure: they can appeal to the executive or legislators or the courts. The whole system might be paralyzed as a result. Political scientist Jonathan Rauch calls this demosclerosis, which he defines as the "progressive loss of the ability to adapt."

Similar concerns surround federalism. In theory, governments will be more creative if we allow subnational entities the freedom to make their own choices. Provinces or states can experiment with different techniques for solving problems. But there is no guarantee that subnational governments will use their freedom in positive ways. They might adopt laws that oppress minorities or gut labour and environmental standards to attract investment. With such problems in mind, the political scientist Harold Laski once condemned federalism as an "inherent foe" of progress.

Federalism also creates the practical difficulty of implementing national policies through two or more levels of government. Even when political leaders at the national and subnational level agree on goals, the costs of administrative coordination may be high. Donald Kettl says federalism in the United States has produced a form of "interwoven administration" for many programs that is "inherently more complicated than direct administration ... [and] more prone to the risks of fraud, waste, abuse and mismanagement; harder to manage; and harder to hold accountable."

Advocates of the FLD model argue coordination problems are offset by the fact that FLD bureaucracies are more closely scrutinized and, therefore, more efficient. But doubts have been raised on that count as well. In the 1990s especially, politicians complained that government agencies were overstaffed and mired in red tape. They pursued many different remedies: replacing civil servants with political appointees, reducing internal regulations, demanding more reports on performance by public agencies, and moving government functions to the private sector. Some complained that the remedies were worse than the disease.

The argument in favour of FLD systems also makes strong assumptions about institutions and practices outside government itself. A well-functioning FLD system requires good schools and universities, a healthy media landscape, associations that can speak effectively for different interests within society, and real choice between political parties.

There is cause for concern on all these fronts. Recent cross-national studies show that young people often leave school with limited knowledge about how government works and do not follow the news as much as previous generations. In many countries, there are fewer journalists covering politics and government because of technological shifts that have devastated old-style media. People do not join community groups or national associations as frequently as they once did, and the share of the private-sector workforce represented by unions has plummeted. Membership in major political parties has declined too. Trust in parties is low throughout the Western world.

THE CENTRAL QUESTION

What should we take from all this? Simply that the adaptability of FLD systems cannot be taken for granted. The adaptability of these systems is a theory, not a fact. We can see how an FLD system might perform the four essential functions of anticipation, redesign, legitimation, and execution, but we can also see many ways in which such a system might break down.

Engineers who are responsible for complicated physical systems sometimes conduct a "failure mode analysis," which is a detailed study of where problems are likely to happen within the system. In a similar fashion, we should perform a failure mode analysis that considers whether political systems are likely to break down in performing the functions essential to adaptability. We want to identify the critical vulnerabilities, where the odds of failure are high and the consequences are substantial.

At the same time, we must recognize that undertaking a failure mode analysis of FLD systems is a difficult task. Too many books offer sweeping statements about Western democracies – or worse still, make generalized statements about democracy based on the experience of one or two systems, such as the United States and the United Kingdom. In reality, though, no two FLD systems are exactly alike. As I show in the next chapter, culture and institutions vary in ways that are critical to adaptability. We must conduct our failure mode analyses one country at a time.

In the next chapter, I look at the Canadian version of the FLD model. I make two arguments. First, I warn against putting Canada and the United States in the same box, so far as adaptability is concerned. There are institutional and cultural differences between the two systems that make some complaints about America's lack of adaptability less relevant to Canada. In the twentieth century, these differences were accentuated because Canadian policy-makers were engaged in a deliberate effort to improve adaptability.

However, the Canadian advantage in adaptability cannot be taken for granted. This is my second argument. I show how developments in the twentieth century have corroded the country's capacity to adapt. Partly, this corrosion is an unintended consequence of reforms undertaken in the late twentieth century, and partly, it has occurred because Canadian leaders no longer think about adaptability as much as they once did.

Canadians should worry about any decline in adaptability. The country is heading into rough waters. The climate emergency has arrived. For this and other reasons, international migration, legal and irregular, is increasing. The Canadian economy is being shaken by radical advances in technology. All of Canada's major partners – the United States, the European Union, India, and China – suffer from declining internal stability. Competition between major powers is intensifying, creating challenges for smaller countries caught in the middle. Some of these developments could aggravate old tensions within Canada. The conditions are ripe for a polycrisis in Canada in the coming decades. A country whose people are not thinking intensively about the future may not survive the coming storm.

2

Canada: Advantages and Dangers

The connection between Canadians and Americans is closer than it was forty years ago. People cross the border more often for work and vacations. They buy more goods and services from, and invest more of their savings in, the country next door. Canadians read and watch more American news and entertainment. The social media networks that have spread like kudzu over the last twenty years ignore national boundaries. Americans post messages on social media, and Canadians like, reply, and repost.

Deeper connections may have encouraged the tendency to regard the two countries as fundamentally alike. Politicians trying to maintain good relations describe Canada and the United States as "sister countries" with "common democratic values" and a "shared cultural heritage." Researchers put "established democracies like Canada and the United States" in the same box, distinct from supposedly shakier regimes in other places.

Canadian politics, meanwhile, seems more and more like an echo of American politics. If a problem dominates the American agenda (ethnonationalism, polarization, racially motivated police violence, vaccine resistance, restrictive abortion laws, culture wars) then fears about that problem intensify in Canada as well. American political and social movements sprout Canadian branches. Some Canadians now believe their system of government is built on the same principles as that of the United States and that it shares the same weaknesses. But the two systems of government are not the same, and the differences are critical when we think about the adaptability of each.

Granted, there is commonality in the abstract. Canada and the United States both have federal-liberal-democratic (FLD) systems of government. At best, each has the potential to function like a sophisticated adaptation machine, as philosophers such as Dewey and Popper once suggested. At worst, each can be compromised by shortsightedness, factionalism, and confusion. In practice, though, the results depend heavily on details: the formal rules that allocate power within an FLD system, the informal practices that guide everyday politics, and the political culture that shapes the behaviour of leaders and citizens.

When we delve into the details, it becomes apparent that, insofar as adaptability is concerned, Canadian FLD governance has advantages over the American version. Or at least it did at the end of the twentieth century. At that time, the Canadian system was better fitted than the American one to perform all the functions that are essential to adaptation: looking ahead to identify new challenges, inventing creative strategies for responding to those challenges, building political support for a path forward, and translating plans into action.

In this chapter, I identify five of those Canadian advantages. Most, but not all, are still in place today. The Canadian state is not as adaptable as it once was. This change is partly the result of Canada's successful social and economic transformation over the last forty years. It has become a more complex and diverse country, in which planning and coordination has become more difficult. Adaptability has also declined because Canadian leaders have taken their eye off the ball. Ways of thinking about politics have changed, and practices that were once essential to adaptability have been abandoned. Canada may teeter on the brink of an adaptability trap: a condition in which large-scale reforms have compromised its capacity for future reforms.

FIXATING ON SURVIVAL

The most important advantage that Canada enjoyed in the twentieth century had nothing to do with the design of institutions. It related more fundamentally to political culture or, in other words, the Canadian way of thinking about politics. Most Canadians were realists, in the sense that they recognized the fragility of the political system and behaved accordingly.

The Canadian preoccupation with fragility has deep roots. Margaret Atwood observed in a now-famous 1972 essay that early Canadian writers were obsessed with survival. They told stories about European settlers struggling against the "savage grip" of an immense and wild territory. "Canadians are forever taking the national pulse like doctors at a sickbed," Atwood said. "The aim is not to see whether the patient will live well but simply whether he will live at all."

For a long time, Canadian politics mirrored its literature. The country created in 1867 was a composite of communities all fixated on survival. Upper Canada (present-day Ontario) was settled by people who fled the American Revolution and who worried for decades afterward about cross-border attacks from the United States. In Lower Canada (Quebec), French-speaking Catholics struggled against a conquering elite that seemed determined to suppress their language and religion. Maritimers sought protection from the United States but also feared domination by Upper and Lower Canada.

Until recently, Canadian historians neglected the most desperate struggle for survival, that of Indigenous peoples. European colonization led to the loss of Indigenous homelands, the division of ancient societies into scattered bands, and socially destructive campaigns by settler governments to "civilize the lesser race." By Confederation, the Indigenous population was a third of what it had been at the time of first contact with Europeans.

The story of Canada since Confederation has largely been about the efforts of these different communities, and others added subsequently, to protect their ways of life. Often, that struggle has been told using the language of sovereignty and self-determination, rather than simple survival. At the same time, Canadian politicians have wrestled with doubts about the survival of the country as a whole, given the centrifugal forces operating within it. The first secessionist movement in Canada arose in Nova Scotia only a few months after Confederation. In the 1920s and 1930s, the overriding concern of Prime Minister William Lyon Mackenzie King was national unity. Lester Pearson said that unity was his "most passionate interest" as prime minister in the mid-1960s. At the end of the twentieth century, Prime Minister Jean Chrétien warned that it was still dangerous to "take Canada for granted."

Canada's survival has been challenged by external as well as internal forces. Fears of an invasion by the United States, stoked by American rhetoric about annexation, persisted until the start of the twentieth century. The next forty years were absorbed by Canada's campaign to achieve independence from Britain, while the decades following World War II were occupied with resistance against the economic and cultural hegemony of the United States. The political philosopher George Grant thought this struggle was a lost cause. In 1967, he mourned "the end of Canada as a sovereign state."

Canada faced other threats in the twentieth century. As a small country, it struggled to maintain its place in a volatile global economy. Economic shocks from abroad often inflamed internal tensions. Canadian leaders seemed "helpless" during the Great Depression of the 1930s, according to political scientist Frank Underhill; they were overwhelmed by "impersonal world forces." The country's top civil servant, O.D. Skelton, warned in 1936 that "the disintegration of Canada is proceeding fast." Anxiety about the "surrender of sovereignty" seized many Canadians as the country integrated into a new global system of liberalized trade and investment after the 1980s.

Before the US Civil War (1861–65), American political culture was permeated by a similar awareness of fragility. American political leaders feared that states might break from the Union or that rivals like Britain would block their country's expansion. This sense of fragility dissipated in the twentieth century. In 1962, President John Kennedy declared that "the old sweeping issues" that once divided the country had evaporated. This confidence about the solidity of the American state persisted at the end of the century. "Never before" in history, President Bill Clinton boasted in 2000, had the United States enjoyed "so little internal crisis and so few external threats."

Of course, few Americans would say that today. The last twenty years have shaken American confidence about the state of their Union. Some prominent Canadians argue that it is Canada, rather than the United States, which now suffers from complacency about its future prospects. If that is true, it would be a sea change from the twentieth century, when one of the critical distinctions between the two countries was the fixation on survival that typified Canadian political culture.

BUILDING THE CAPACITY TO LOOK AHEAD

An awareness of fragility is a necessary condition for adaptability because it heightens alertness to potential dangers. But alertness is not enough. An adaptable country must have methods for gauging the severity of threats, crafting potential responses, and building consensus about the path forward.

In any liberal democracy, much of this work is done by elements of civil society, including citizens, journalists, associations, and universities. Canadian civil society was hobbled throughout the twentieth century by a small population, limited resources, and the loss of talent to global metropoles, such as London and New York. Canadian governments compensated for these problems by making their own investments in the country's capacity for forward-thinking. This was another distinctive feature of Canadian governance in the latter half of the twentieth century. Political scientist David Smith said it separated Canada from the United States. Canadians, Smith said in 1995, were "an inquiring people."

Smith was thinking about our penchant for establishing commissions of inquiry throughout the twentieth century. There are two types of commissions. One type, still frequently used today, investigates misconduct in government. These inquiries look backward at events to uncover what went wrong. They often seem like trials, replete with lawyers, witnesses, and findings of guilt. These backward-looking inquiries are not of interest for this analysis. We are more interested in the second type of inquiry, which looks forward rather than backward. Commonly known as royal commissions, these inquiries explore national problems and craft possible solutions.

Royal commissions are as old as the country itself. But in the mid-twentieth century, they took on a new form and significance. The precedent was set by the Royal Commission on Dominion-Provincial Relations, also known as the Rowell-Sirois Commission because of its co-chairs, which was established in 1937 to reconsider the roles of federal and provincial governments given their feeble response to the Great Depression. Rowell-Sirois was more ambitious than earlier commissions. It hired a "staff of experts representing the best scholarship of Canada," consulted with federal and provincial officials, received briefs from the public, and held hearings across the country. Its final report, a compendium of history, analysis, and statistics, was seven hundred pages long, and there were background papers too. Political scientist Donald Smiley called it "the most exhaustive investigation of a governmental system that has ever been made."

The Rowell-Sirois report had a profound influence on the evolution of federalism after World War II. Just as important, it improved public understanding of how government worked and also – in the words of one 1940 commentator – "the kind of world in which we are likely to be living" in the post-war era. The report became a bestseller at a dollar a copy. Ryerson Press produced a short version with "all the average man needs to know" about its findings.

Rowell-Sirois provided a template for national problem solving after World War II. The same method – background studies, public hearings, a final report – was used by the Gordon Commission, whose 1957 report explored Canada's economic prospects for the next quarter-century. Simon Kuznets, a Nobel Prize economist, suggested that the commission's recommendations might have been the least important aspect of its work. The commission improved knowledge, educated the public, and provided a "balanced framework within which policy decisions can be made." The commission's work shaped the Canadian debate on economic policy for the next twenty years.

In the 1960s, the report of the Carter Commission on taxation won international praise as "a landmark ... [and] a model for the world to follow." And in 1982, the federal government launched the most ambitious inquiry yet, the Macdonald Commission, whose report and three hundred background studies laid the groundwork for a sea change in Canadian economic policy in the last quarter of the twentieth century. The commission's aim, Macdonald later explained, was to consider "where Canadians were going as a nation, as well as the great events that were going to shape the world around them."

Royal commissions were not limited to the economy. They helped to lay the foundation for the Canadian welfare state (the Hall Commission, which reported in 1964), equality for French-speaking Canadians (the Laurendeau-Dunton Commission, 1967) and for women (the Bird Commission, 1970), and justice for Indigenous peoples (the Berger Commission, 1977, and the Royal Commission on Aboriginal Peoples, 1996).

Royal commissions, "marked, if not inspired, some of the pivotal moments in Canada's modern history." Their recommendations were not always adopted. But as Kuznets suggested in 1959, this is not the correct standard for judging their work. Royal commissions were tools for mobilizing the country's intellectual resources. They focused attention on critical problems, supported scholarly research, structured the national conversation, and improved public understanding. Choices were defined for public debate, even if recommendations were not immediately adopted. As Thomas Berger said in 1977, commissions "added to ... Canada's storefront of ideas."

After World War II, Canadian governments refined another tool for forward-thinking: the independent advisory council. In 1962, the Conservative government led by John Diefenbaker established a National Council of Welfare to provide advice on social policy. Its role was expanded by the Trudeau government seven years later. Diefenbaker also set up a National Productivity Council to address problems of economic development. It was transformed into the

Economic Council of Canada (ECC) by the Pearson government in 1963. The Pearson government saw the ECC as something like an ongoing royal commission, designed to "contemplate the future in a comprehensive way." Safeguards were put in place to protect the ECC's independence. By the early 1990s, it was the largest think tank, public or private, in Canada.

The ECC was not alone. The Science Council of Canada, created in 1966, gave advice on long-term objectives for the development and use of science and technology and promoted public awareness of challenges in technological development. Four years later, the Law Reform Commission was created to provide "an overall view of the legal system in Canada." And in 1972, the federal government launched another independent body, the Institute for Research on Public Policy, to promote "long-term research and thinking … into governmental matters of all kinds." Several other councils were created over the next twenty years.

PROTECTING THE PUBLIC SPHERE

People who promote the FLD model as a machine for inventing solutions to national problems and building support for national strategy assume the existence of a healthy public sphere. "Public sphere" is a term coined by the philosopher Jürgen Habermas to describe a realm in which members of a community deliberate about the use of power within that community.Others prefer to talk about a "shared public space." The public sphere encompasses all the ways that citizens talk with one another about public affairs, from broadcast television to social media to neighbourhood meetings. Without a healthy public sphere, citizens have no way of sharing and testing ideas, and no way of resolving their differences.

In the twentieth century, the United States had enough people and money that the existence of a public sphere could be taken for granted. There were large markets to support newspapers, magazines, and radio and television stations. Canadian policy-makers were not so lucky. It was harder for Canadians to talk with one another because the population was smaller, more dispersed, divided by language, and often drowned out by loud American neighbours.

In a fundamental sense, Canadians at the start of the twentieth century lacked the capacity to think for themselves. "Too often our convictions are borrowed from London, Paris, or New York," a group of Canadian writers complained in 1920. "Real independence" required that the country have the capacity to manufacture its own "faith and philosophy." These writers proposed to do this by starting a magazine, *The Canadian Forum*, which continued publishing for the next eighty years. Its launch was accompanied by a national movement that organized community meetings called People's Forums to promote understanding of Canadian public affairs. Canadians were fretting about the public sphere well before Habermas invented the phrase.

Concern about the health of the public sphere was a leitmotif of twentieth-century Canadian politics. Some Canadian academics became internationally famous for their work on this subject. Their general theme was that the public sphere was something that had to be nurtured carefully. Left alone, technological developments and market forces were potentially destructive. In 1946, political scientist Robert MacIver warned that "modern means of communication" could be exploited by "unscrupulous interests, indifferent to truth," who preyed on "blind emotions and prejudices." Four years later, Harold Innis published a pathbreaking book explaining how new communication technologies often undermined the ability of people to think clearly about politics. In the 1960s, Marshall McLuhan predicted the arrival of an electronic "global village" in which "everything affects everything all the time." This new world was alluring, McLuhan conceded, but it would also be plagued by "panic terrors."

Constructing and maintaining a healthy public sphere was also a principal concern of Canadian governments for most of the twentieth century. The arrival of radio in the 1920s led to the Aird Commission, which warned that a purely commercial broadcasting system would neglect public affairs and promote "ideals and opinions that are not Canadian." The advent of television in the 1950s led to the Massey Commission, a broad survey of the state of Canadian culture, which concluded that Canadian sovereignty was becoming "an empty shell" because of an American media "invasion."

The dire health of Canada's magazine industry was examined by the 1961 O'Leary Commission, which warned that "communications are the thread which binds together the fibers of a nation ... [They] are as vital to its life as its defences, and should receive at least as great a measure of national protection." The shuttering of newspapers in the 1970s led to the Kent Commission, which predicted that the industry would soon be upended by a technological revolution. Canadians needed help in managing a blizzard of information, the commission warned, but newspapers might not survive to perform that function.

Governments not only studied the public sphere. They also took measures to protect it, using every tool imaginable. The federal government began by subsidizing the distribution of newspapers and magazines by mail. It followed this initial action with the establishment of the Canadian Broadcasting Corporation in 1936. In the post–World War II era, the federal government added restrictions on foreign ownership of media companies, limits on the re-broadcasting of foreign-produced shows, bans on the importation of foreign magazines, tax incentives for advertisers to support Canadian media, and cash grants to support the production of Canadian news and culture.

This bundle of interventions did not always work well. But imagine how much worse off Canada would have been in the twentieth century if none of these measures had been adopted. The country would have lacked the capacity to chart its own course, to test ideas and forge agreement on national strategy, just as the editors of *The Canadian Forum* warned in 1920. Adaptability would have been compromised as a result.

ENERGETIC EXECUTIVES

Adaptable systems are those that look for dangers, invent strategies for managing those dangers, and build agreement on the best path forward. There is also a fourth requirement. Governments must have the ability to translate strategy into action. Practically, this means that governments must have the ability to adopt new laws and enforce them, to tax and spend, and to restructure governmental agencies so that they address new problems.

This is one area in which the Canadian system has a clear advantage over that of the United States. The Canadian system gives the prime minister and premiers of provinces and territories – otherwise known as first ministers – the power to move more decisively than American presidents and governors. During debates on the American constitution in the 1780s, Alexander Hamilton argued that "energy in the Executive is a leading character in the definition of good government." But Hamilton was on the losing side of that argument. Energetic executives are a feature of Canadian but not American government.

Of course, there are dangers within a strong-executive system. Canadians spend a lot of time devising checks against potential abuses of executive power. One Liberal member of Parliament, Anthony Housefather, even suggested in 2022 that Canada would be better off with the American form of government. But the American system suffers from even bigger frailties. It is prone to dysfunctionality, as many American critics have said. Timely and coherent action is often impossible. Within a superpower like the United States, the consequences of dysfunctionality can be borne for a long time. In a country like Canada, dysfunctionality could easily be fatal.

The main reason that Canadian first ministers are relatively powerful is that we follow the parliamentary system of government. A nineteenth-century observer of the parliamentary system, Walter Bagehot, noted that it partly fuses executive and legislative powers, rather than completely separating them as the Americans do. On important questions, Canadian first ministers know they have the support of a majority within the main legislative chamber. In other words, divided government is impossible in Canada.

This is not true in the United States, where presidents and governors are elected separately from legislatures. A situation in which the two branches are controlled by different parties is increasingly common in Washington and American state capitals. The risk of divided government is compounded in the United States because the legislative branch almost always has two popularly elected chambers. This arrangement is called bicameralism. (The sole exception is Nebraska, which eliminated its upper chamber in 1936.) At the federal level in the United States, these two chambers are the House of Representatives and the Senate, which together comprise the Congress.

Canadian government rejects the principle of bicameralism almost entirely, which simplifies life for first ministers and their Cabinets. No provincial government has an upper chamber. While the federal parliament includes an upper chamber, the Senate, this body has a limited role. As the Supreme Court of Canada explained in 2014, the Senate was not designed to be a coequal or rival of the House of Commons. The Senate may push for reconsideration of bills from the House of Commons that are "hasty or ill-considered" but lacks authority to "systematically block" the will of the House.

In the United States, by contrast, bicameralism has teeth. To achieve unified government, a political party must win control of the executive branch and both legislative chambers. Americans call this the trifecta. In Washington, the trifecta has been achieved in just twelve of the last forty years. Only once has a trifecta lasted for more than twenty-four months. Policy-making in the United States is heavily shaped by the transience of trifectas. Presidents and governors rush to pass major new laws while conditions are favourable, and especially in the few months immediately after their inauguration. This behaviour stokes polarization and often results in poorly drafted laws. When trifectas evaporate, governance becomes even more challenging. At the extreme, the executive may be compelled to stop work because the legislature refuses to provide funding, as Congress has done ten times since 1980. Shutdowns like this are unknown in Canada.

Executive authority within American state governments is constrained in two additional ways. Most states have a plural executive, a system in which several key officials other than the governor, such as the treasurer and attorney general, are directly elected. There is no guarantee that all these officials will represent the same party, and partisan competition within the executive branch is commonplace. Most governors also face restrictions on taxing, spending, and borrowing. Their capacity to invest in long-term initiatives, or provide relief during economic downturns, is limited. Poor states are further constrained because Washington does not provide equalization payments, as Ottawa does for poorer provinces.

Adaptability in the Canadian system is also enhanced by distinctive practices relating to the delegation of authority from the legislative branch to the executive branch. Canadian legislators often lay out general principles in statutes and allow public servants to fill in the details by making regulations. This practice allows flexibility to resolve problems that were not anticipated when a law was drafted, and to make adjustments as circumstances change.

By contrast, American laws are generally longer and more detailed. Legislators add details because they do not trust the executive branch to follow their wishes. They also impose more complex procedures for making regulations. One result is that interest groups have more opportunities to obstruct regulation-making by government agencies. Fixing unexpected problems with regulations, or updating them to meet new conditions, is harder in the American system.

There is one kind of power delegation from legislature to executive that is especially important. It has to do with the reorganization of government agencies. Shuffling boxes within the governmental organization chart is an essential task as priorities change. Restructuring is easier in Canada because broad discretion over the organization of the executive is given to the prime minister, acting on advice of senior officials. Most departments in Canada's federal government are less than thirty years old, and the average age of departments is less than fifty years.

The situation is different in the United States. Congress exercises tight control over the creation or dissolution of departments and also determines their internal structure. One result is that bureaucratic reorganization within American government is a less common and more painful process. There are fifteen executive departments within the US government. Only one has been created in the last thirty years, and the average age of departments is more than one hundred years.

Finally, Canada's political leaders are advantaged by having a different kind of bureaucracy than their American counterparts. The difference is especially marked for the higher civil service – the three or four top layers of the bureaucracy. In Canada, these positions are routinely filled by public servants who have spent most of their careers in government. In the United States, they are filled by political appointees, who serve at the pleasure of the president and leave when the president does. In Washington, every new president must make about four thousand appointments, a quarter of which must also be approved by the Senate.

At first glance, the American system seems to give presidents more control over the bureaucracy. But the benefits are overestimated and the costs immense. Transitions between presidents are complicated because of the massive turnover of critical personnel. The system is especially vulnerable to crises during transitions. Backlogs in the appointment process mean that hundreds of positions remain vacant even a year after a president's inauguration. The lack of personnel in key positions causes drift and confusion within agencies. Frequently, political appointees are unqualified for their jobs. Agencies led by appointees perform poorly relative to those run by career civil servants, even by the standards set by presidents themselves. In some situations, such as Hurricane Katrina in 2005, the incompetence of appointees has had disastrous results.

COORDINATING GOVERNMENTAL ACTION

In theory, a federal system improves adaptability for two reasons: because there is more room for experimentation by governments and because one level of government functions as a backup if another level fails. But adaptability might also be compromised in a federal system, especially when both national and subnational governments are led by energetic executives. Governments can march in opposite directions, so that action by one government undermines action by another. Governments might also fail to co-operate in executing policies that depend on joint action. Left unattended, small differences between governments can fester into deep grievances that undermine the capacity to talk about shared challenges.

To preserve adaptability, a federal system needs mechanisms for avoiding these problems. There must be a process that encourages national and subnational leaders to talk about national strategy, so that leaders share common goals or at least understand exactly where they disagree. This dialogue must continue even when governments have sharp differences. In addition, there must be procedures for information sharing and coordination among lower-level officials in national and subnational agencies.

Arrangements like these are the essential connective tissue of a federal system. They hold the bones of the system together and allow the whole structure to move in a smooth and orchestrated way. But Canada's first constitutional law, the British North America Act of 1867, was largely silent on the question of how federal and provincial governments would work with one another.

In the twentieth century, Canadian policy-makers remedied this deficiency by building a sophisticated apparatus for intergovernmental relations (IGR). This apparatus worked at three levels. At the top were meetings of first ministers. These became routine after World War II. K.C. Wheare, an internationally recognized expert on federalism in the post-war era, said in 1968 that first ministers' meetings were an "outstanding" technique for achieving flexibility within the Canadian system, allowing it to "adapt to the changing needs of the time." One level down were regular meetings of ministers who were responsible for specific policy areas, such as finance or the environment. At the third level were routine interactions among federal and provincial public servants working in the same area.

Every Canadian government hired officials to specialize in intergovernmental relations, and offices were established whose only purpose was to manage intergovernmental meetings. One of these offices, the Canadian Intergovernmental Conference Secretariat, has hosted almost five thousand meetings since its creation in 1973.

In 1973, political scientist Richard Simeon said that Canada had invented a distinctive system of federal–provincial diplomacy, similar in many ways to the diplomatic machinery for managing relations between independent countries. Simeon observed that the IGR apparatus depended on political culture as much as institutions. It worked because leaders thought about national politics in a certain way. John Courtney had the same idea in mind when he observed in 1969 that "governing Canada is an exercise as much in diplomacy as in politics."

The diplomatic style emphasized constant engagement, restraint, and accommodation. Prime Minister Wilfrid Laurier was describing the diplomatic style when he said in 1911 that "moderation and conciliation" was the "policy of true Canadianism" and when he admitted that his general approach to politics was to say as little as possible about "exciting subjects." Seventy years later, Ontario Premier Bill Davis responded to criticism of his own anodyne ways by insisting, "bland works." Saskatchewan Attorney General John Whyte endorsed the diplomatic style when he told the Supreme Court of Canada in 1995 that the country was woven from "the threads of a thousand acts of accommodation."

Saying that Canadian political culture in the twentieth century emphasized diplomacy is not the same as saying that Canadian leaders always got along. On the contrary, diplomacy was emphasized because leaders did not get along. Canadian governments were frequently at loggerheads, and sometimes leaders disliked one another intensely. Divisions were so deep that they periodically threatened the survival of the country. This is why the diplomatic style was emphasized. It was treatment for a potentially fatal condition of the Canadian system.

The Canadian approach to intergovernmental relations in the post–World War II era differed substantially from the American approach. There is no comparable IGR apparatus in the United States, partly because power in every American government is divided between chief executives and bicameral legislatures and also because the higher levels of federal and state bureaucracies are filled with political appointees. The intergovernmental game in the United States includes more players, many of whom are only in the game for a short time. This means that the game is more chaotic. There is no stable agenda, and it is harder to make long-term plans. Players are less likely to know each other or to understand the history of intergovernmental conflicts.

Added to this is a critical difference in political culture between Canada and the United States. There was a period in American history when leaders were acutely aware of regional divisions and also emphasized conciliation and compromise, just as Canadians did in the late twentieth century. But that era ended in the United States in the early twentieth century. After that time, American leaders began taking national unity for granted. Consequently, they had less motivation to build institutions for managing conflict among federal and state governments.

Of course, conditions in the United States have changed over the last quarter-century. Today, political polarization in the United States is driven by policy disagreements that are largely rooted in geography. People in different regions of the country have clashing views about government and society that American political institutions, as they have evolved over the last century, are not well designed to manage. The United States has caught the Canadian disease but lacks medicine for treating it.

CHANGES SINCE 1980

We should not be sentimental about Canadian politics in the twentieth century. For most of that century, the system had glaring weaknesses. It shut out women, francophones, racialized minorities, and 2SLGBTQI+ persons. It denied the rights of Indigenous peoples and suppressed Indigenous cultures. Government was often clubby, secretive, and hostile to public participation. Government policies were frequently wrong-headed and ineffective. But the system had a capacity for adaptation, and it did adapt. The political system that operates in Canada today differs in fundamental ways from the system that operated in 1980.

A bigger and more diverse population. Most fundamentally, the system includes more people. Canada's population has grown by 60 per cent since 1980, from twenty-five million to forty million people. From the point of view of 1980, that is like adding another Ontario and another Quebec to the federation. This growth rate was three times faster than the average for all developed countries during the same period of time. It was not an accident but the intended result of more liberal immigration policies. Today, almost one out of four Canadians is an immigrant. Most now come from Asia rather than Europe. The Canadian polity is more diverse in terms of culture, faith, language, and racialized identity.

Empowered individuals. Citizens enjoy more freedom than they did in 1980. The Canadian Charter of Rights and Freedoms, adopted in 1982, limits the ability of governments to regulate private life. Rights established within the Charter have been amplified by decisions of the Supreme Court of Canada. At the same time, federal and provincial governments have adopted laws that affirm the right to privacy and the right to be protected against discrimination based on race, sexual orientation, gender identity, and other characteristics.

Individual empowerment is a matter of cultural as well as legal change. Canadians are better educated than they were in 1980, more aware of their rights, and less trusting of government. They have the motivation and technological tools to organize rapidly in defence of their freedoms. Canadians also have higher expectations about their role in formulating government policies. For example, the 1982 constitutional reforms were completed without a national referendum. That would be unimaginable today.

Empowered provinces. Power has shifted from Ottawa to provincial and territorial capitals. The federal government accounts for a smaller share of total government spending than it did in 1982. This change is partly the result of growth in programs that fall mainly under provincial jurisdiction, such as education and health care. Provinces have also pushed successfully for a more substantial role in areas of shared jurisdiction, such as immigration.

Quebec led the movement for more provincial authority, arguing that this change was necessary to protect its own language and culture. The province's negotiating position was strengthened by the near success of separatists in the 1995 referendum on secession. In 1998, the

Supreme Court of Canada acknowledged that there is a path to independence for Quebec if a referendum within the province produces a clear mandate. By implication, the same path can be followed by other provinces. In 2000, Parliament recognized the path to independence as well. The House of Commons recognized the Québécois as a distinct nation within Canada in 2006.

Leaders in other provinces have tried to emulate Quebec. In 2021, Premier Scott Moe declared that Saskatchewan was also "a nation within a nation" and promised to make the province "stronger and more independent." In 2022, Premier Danielle Smith promised to defend the "unique culture and shared identity" of Albertans by obstructing the enforcement of federal laws.

Liberated markets. Government's role in the economy has been transformed as well. In the 1980s, Canada abandoned a decades-old policy of protectionism and embraced free trade with the United States. In following years, it extended the policy of free trade to other countries. New international tribunals were created to settle trade disputes without interference by national politicians. A similar system was created to promote free trade among Canadian provinces and territories.

Meanwhile the federal government removed limits on investment by foreign corporations and sold government-owned companies like Air Canada, Canadian National Railways, and Petro-Canada. Controls on major industries, including telecommunications and airlines, were loosened, and federal authorities stopped attempting to control the exchange rate for the Canadian dollar. Politicians affirmed the independence of the Bank of Canada and gave it the mission of preventing a resurgence of the high inflation of the 1970s.

Empowering of Indigenous peoples. Over the last forty years, Indigenous peoples have made progress in regaining control over their lands and communities. The 1982 Constitution Act acknowledges the long-neglected treaty rights of Indigenous peoples. In a series of decisions, the Supreme Court has insisted that governments deal honourably with First Nations and consult them when Indigenous interests are affected by government action. In 2021, the federal government affirmed a United Nations declaration that prohibits actions affecting Indigenous communities without their prior and informed consent.

Federal and provincial authorities have been criticized for obstructing Indigenous land claims with litigation and slowness in devolving authority to Indigenous governments. Still, more than twenty major agreements have been concluded by the federal government. The largest of Canada's provinces and territories, Nunavut, was created as a result of a settlement with the Inuit Tapiriit Kanatami in 1993. Experts describe these changes as an "Indigenous governance revolution."

Reconciliation with Indigenous peoples also requires acknowledgment of past injustices. A 2015 inquiry concluded that the federal government had engaged in a program of cultural genocide against Indigenous peoples for more than a century. Other reports have exposed human rights violations against Indigenous women and chronic failure to provide Indigenous communities with clean water, health care, and education. These reports have battered Ottawa's credibility and bolstered demands for faster devolution of power.

More accountable government. The structure of government in Ottawa has changed in fundamental ways since 1980. Some commentators emphasize the ways in which power has been concentrated in the hands of the prime minister and his advisers. This trend is undeniable. But there have also been trends in the other direction. In several ways, executive power is more constrained than it was forty years ago. For example, prime ministers are less likely to oversee majority governments. Elections are fought more fiercely today.

There are also more external checks on the executive branch. The Supreme Court scrutinizes executive action more closely than it once did. Reforms to the Senate have made it a more independent and competent overseer of government policy. And Parliament has appointed a phalanx of independent watchdogs to report on the executive branch's performance with regard to fiscal discipline, efficiency, transparency, privacy, official languages, ethics, and environmental sustainability. Ottawa has invented a new system of "monitory democracy" that is anchored by these watchdogs.

The federal bureaucracy has also been renovated, and in many ways constrained, since 1980. It is roughly the same size as forty years ago. However, this means that the ratio of federal workers to citizens has declined substantially. Government work is increasingly done at other levels of government. The public service is now more representative of the general population. It is also more tightly bound by rules designed to improve fairness, transparency, and accountability in decision-making.

Meanwhile the number of political staff whose job is to enforce the will of ministers has ballooned. Senior public servants are moved between assignments more frequently, with the result that their knowledge and control of departments is weakened. There is a strong sense that top-level public servants no longer influence government policy as they once did.

In sum, the Canadian way of governing has changed dramatically over the span of four decades. A new grand strategy has emerged that reflects new understandings about national priorities and the best ways of achieving those priorities, and that has been made concrete by renovated institutions and practices. There is a remarkable level of agreement on this grand strategy. Few Canadians would argue that any of the changes I have just described should be wholly reversed. And for the most part, these reforms have made Canada a better place to live – more just, more prosperous, more democratic.

But what about adaptability? After all of these renovations, does Canada's political system still have the capacity to anticipate and manage threats to the survival and health of the system as a whole?

ADAPTABILITY AT RISK

There is good reason to worry about adaptability. Look back at the list of changes to the Canadian system over the last forty years. Overall, these changes have made the system larger, more complex, and more decentralized. There are many more people in the country, and there is a larger flow of immigrants. The pace of economic activity has increased, with more transactions occurring every day. Power has been distributed more widely within the system – to individuals, provinces and territories, Indigenous communities, and private businesses. And national borders have blurred, so that the attention of citizens, businesses, and governments is pulled in more directions. How, in this new and more complicated reality, do we assure that everyone is paying attention to the long run, and how do we encourage everyone to act in complementary ways to address long-term hazards?

This question has been neglected in Canada for the last quarter-century. For good reasons, the political system was restructured. This successful transformation is a testament to the adaptability of the system as it stood in the late twentieth century. The irony, though, is that all this restructuring may have compromised the government's adaptive capacity itself. I call this the adaptability trap: a predicament in which reforms limit the possibility of further reforms.

In Canada, this predicament has arisen largely because policy-makers took their eye off the ball, insofar as adaptability is concerned. While they made the system larger and more complex, they neglected institutions and practices that are necessary to maintain a focus on long-term challenges, build consensus on national strategy, and ensure timely and coordinated execution of that strategy.

In the next chapter, I demonstrate how Canadian national politics increasingly prioritizes short-term considerations over long-term planning. While politicians and public servants may address specific issues with a long-term perspective, their ability to formulate and articulate comprehensive strategies for national challenges has waned. Officials are consumed by immediate political demands, leaving little room for debate about broader, long-term strategy. At the same time, institutions that once served as a bulwark against short-termism have been dismantled. Quite deliberately, Ottawa chose to spend less time on formulating national strategy for the long run.

The capacity of Canada's leaders to deliberate over national strategy, and formulate a common view about the best path forward for the country, has also been compromised. In chapter 4, I show how this shift is also the result of deliberate choices made by both Liberal and Conservative prime ministers. First ministers do not convene regularly as they once did, and even when they do, Indigenous leaders may not be included. In the late 1990s and early 2000s, avoiding first minister meetings seemed like a good way of cooling down national politics. Today, however, refusal to meet routinely contributes to drift and confusion in the national dialogue about grand strategy.

This erosion of dialogue among Canada's leaders is mirrored by a decline in the capacity of the general public to engage in conversation about national priorities. As I show in chapter 5, technological change has upended the Canadian public sphere. New technologies have radically improved access to information and empowered social movements, but they have also reduced the potential for focused, rational discussions on national priorities. Missteps by government have compounded the damage done by technological innovations. Schools in Canada put too little emphasis on civic and historical education. Attempts to safeguard the public sphere have been ad hoc and ineffectual.

Strategy is worthless without efficient execution, and execution hinges on well-functioning bureaucracies. Here again, there is cause for concern. In chapter 6, I explore growing apprehensions about the agility of federal departments and agencies. Over decades, controls have been layered on federal public service, often for good reasons but without sufficient scrutiny of the controls' cumulative effect on bureaucratic performance. Because of this and other problems, an exhaustive, independent evaluation of the public service's role and structure is urgently required. Such reviews were once routine but were abandoned at the end of the twentieth century.

There are many ways of remedying the problems that I describe in this book. In chapter 7, I suggest reforms that could enhance adaptability within Canada's political system. Briefly, I suggest that Ottawa should:

- bolster the capacity of political parties to think in a sophisticated way about long-run challenges and inform citizens about options for national policy

- establish a routine of national leaders' conferences that include all first ministers and Indigenous leaders, working from a commonly agreed-upon and public agenda

- develop a more focused and coherent approach to maintaining the health of the Canadian public sphere and reorganize the federal bureaucracy accordingly

- establish a royal commission to review the role of Canada's political and public services and to consider whether they are designed to fulfill that role for the next thirty years

None are these reforms are radical or expensive, and they do not require difficult constitutional changes. Together, though, they would improve the odds that Canada will survive and thrive in the tumult of the twenty-first century.

3

Short-Term Politics

In chapter 1, I outlined the four requirements of an adaptable system. The first is that a system should be capable of anticipating dangers, and the second is that it should be capable of formulating a strategy for meeting them. Not just one or another of those dangers but all of them since they might arrive at the same time and compound into a polycrisis. Political culture and institutions together must encourage vigilance and planning for anticipated dangers. In Canada today, however, vigilance and planning are in decline. Politics is increasingly focused on controversies of the moment.

All political systems struggle to some extent with forward planning. One long-standing problem is distraction. Leaders and citizens can become preoccupied by everyday events, especially when government is not good at resolving smaller problems efficiently. Decision-makers can be overwhelmed by the demands of the moment. Pierre Trudeau had this problem in mind in 1970, when he compared politicians in Ottawa to "Coney Island cowboys, just shooting at targets as they appear, rushing from one urgent thing to another thing, never finding time to look at the non-urgent but extraordinarily important questions which would become urgent in three or five years."

In democratic systems, there is added pressure to neglect the long run. This is an old criticism against democracy: that politicians, hustling for power, worry more about the next election than they do about the next thirty years. "'Let the morrow provide for itself,'" a nineteenth-century writer said, "is the most likely maxim of the minister of a democracy." This problem of "democratic myopia" has obsessed economists for decades. Elected leaders seemed to prefer pre-election spending binges over thoughtful long-term investments.

In Canada, as we have seen, there were countervailing tendencies at work in the late twentieth century that tended to check the influence of distraction and democratic myopia. Political culture emphasized the fragility of the system in the face of internal and external pressures, and sometimes this pushed politicians and citizens toward a longer and broader view of national challenges. At the same time, governments set up institutions like royal commissions and independent advisory councils that acted as an imperfect control on short-termism.

In the twenty-first century, however, several dangerous trends are at work, intensifying the twin problems of distraction and myopia. Social and technological transformations are turning Ottawa into more of a pressure cooker, in which politicians are overwhelmed by events and left with little time to think about grand strategy. Meanwhile, rising political instability has led politicians to fixate more on the next election. To survive in this environment, Canadian parties have developed a mode of campaigning and governing that emphasizes the publication and implementation of detailed party platforms. This new style of platform governance has corroded political culture and policymaking in Ottawa.

At the same time, Ottawa has abandoned institutions that were once used to check short-termism. It has disinvested in forward-thinking, and organizations outside government have been unable to fill this gap. There are still government departments and agencies that worry about the long run in their specific areas of expertise, such as the environment, national defence, or foreign relations. But the capacity to take an integrated view of grand strategy for the next generation has been weakened. Ottawa has reverted to a kind of politics that is unduly preoccupied with controversies of the moment.

THE INCREASING PRESSURE OF EVENTS

Pierre Trudeau used a second metaphor when he described Ottawa politics at a Liberal Party conference in Harrison Hot Springs in 1969. "We are like the pilots of a supersonic airplane," Trudeau said. "By the time an airport comes into the pilot's field of vision, it is too late to begin the landing procedure." Trudeau was describing the rush of events that made it hard to think about the big picture. He hoped his new government would rise above the maelstrom, but it had limited success in doing this. In the 1970s, ministers in the Liberal government of Pierre Trudeau faced a "constant avalanche of problems." Michael Pitfield, head of the federal public service from 1975 to 1979 and again from 1980 to 1982, observed that time had become one of the scarcest resources in Ottawa. Trudeau's ministers struggled to keep up with their work. A historian described them as "men and women worn down by the weight of their tasks." Circumstances did not improve with the advent of a Conservative government in the 1980s. John Crosbie, a Conservative minister from 1984 to 1993, said that the pressure of work was "unbelievable."

The load on ministers has intensified since then, for several reasons. Canadian society has become bigger and more complex. The economy is three times larger than in the early 1980s, and there are sixteen million more citizens. This population is more diverse and more demanding. Partly this is because they are better educated. Fewer than one million Canadians had a university degree in the early 1970s, while today the number exceeds ten million. Citizens are more aware of their rights and less trusting of politicians. In some quarters, alienation from federal government is profound.

Globalization has also complicated life in Ottawa. Canada trades more extensively with a larger number of countries and depends more heavily on foreign investment. Three out of ten Canadians were born in another country, and four million Canadian citizens live elsewhere. Millions of businesspeople and tourists cross Canadian borders every year. In a world like this, the range of shocks that can be felt in Ottawa is widened. Viruses, financial crises, and inflationary pressures jump borders almost instantaneously. Canadian government policy hinges on the mood of New York bankers and party cadres in Beijing. Domestic controversies in other countries quickly become controversies for diasporic communities in Canada too.

Radical improvements in communication technologies have ramped up pressure as well. Decision-makers are deluged with news, and problems demand an immediate response. In 2010, former British prime minister Tony Blair said that the pace of modern politics was "a planet away from that of even twenty years ago … Decisions have to be made, positions taken, strategies worked out and communicated with a speed that is the speed of light compared to the speed of sound." Gaffes and contradictions in ministerial statements are exposed instantly.

New technologies have empowered citizens and made them less amenable to influence. As the Rouleau inquiry observed, protests like the 2022 Freedom Convoy can "organize at a previously unachievable rate and scale." Citizens with strong views on controversial topics routinely barrage government officials with thousands of emails. But citizens themselves are also overwhelmed by a tsunami of information. Government officials struggle to be heard in a world where the attention of citizens has become a scarcer resource.

Electoral pressures have intensified too. The proportion of Canadians who can be counted as loyal party supporters has declined over the decades. "Voters are promiscuous," Gerald Butts, a former adviser to Prime Minister Justin Trudeau, said in 2023. "Party adhesion is very weak in Canada." The result is a world of unstable politics in which leaders can take nothing for granted. The Progressive Conservative Party that dominated Parliament in the 1980s collapsed in the 1990s. The Liberal Party that governed from 1993 to 2005 was pronounced dead in 2011, only to recover power four years later. The New Democratic Party rose from 19 seats in the House of Commons in 2004 to 103 seats in 2011, plummeting to 24 seats in 2019. Intensified competition has caused all parties to sharpen their operations. Parties are more centralized, disciplined, and technologically sophisticated. Campaigns once run by semi-amateurs are dominated today by professional strategists, pollsters, and marketers.

Scholars in other countries sometimes blame short-term thinking on "electoral cycles": the reality that politicians are focused on an election calendar that is fixed in the constitution. In Canada, however, there is no fixed electoral cycle. The Canadian Constitution does not specify the exact period between elections, although there is a rule that the period cannot exceed five years. For recent Canadian governments, there has rarely been a guarantee that their tenure would last even that long. For most of the twenty-first century, no single party has held a majority in the House of Commons, and opposition parties might force an election at any time. Ministers worked on the assumption that elections could happen on short notice.

Political instability has increased the likelihood that ministers will lack experience in managing all these pressures. Most of the Liberal Cabinet appointed after the 2015 election had never served in Parliament before. "It was a little bit like when you see kindergarten children all tied up with ropes, going down the street," recalled Marc Garneau, the new transport minister. Members of the new Cabinet also faced an extraordinary workload. Justice minister Jody Wilson-Raybould recalled that the typical workday during the first Trudeau government was "grinding": "My ministerial days were long, seemingly endless, filled with countless piles of paper, and crammed with so many meetings that they truly blurred together. As I became more accustomed to my role, the days only got longer, and it felt like sleep disappeared altogether … In all the years I was minister I never had a spare moment. My life was scheduled to the minute … There was never-ending reading … Also endless was the overwhelming volume of correspondence … Everything was always presented as urgent, and much of it truly was."

Wilson-Raybould's experience in Cabinet was not unusual. A former head of the federal public service, Michael Wernick, warned prospective ministers in 2021 that they would face "a constant struggle to keep up" and that "burnout and weariness" would eventually set in. Political staff who support ministers also confront "long work hours that cause people to burn out." Staff working on issues management for Prime Minister Stephen Harper were usually at their desks before five o'clock in the morning. A 2016 study also described workdays beginning in the pre-dawn hours, with staff "trying to figure out when to get in the shower because the conversations are so intense." In 2023, noting the pressure of social media, a former staffer said: "It's no wonder people burn out more and more … Twitter is not real life, but boy it affects your life."

The world that ministers and staff describe is one in which deliberation about the future is immensely difficult. The volume of work does not permit it. The priority is getting business done, avoiding or remedying gaffes, and preparing for the next election. As former finance minister Bill Morneau observed, "your ability to focus on the long-term" is compromised by the demands of the moment. In 2023, government house leader Mark Holland described the pressure on Ottawa politicians to work eighty or ninety hours a week and asked, "Where do you get the time to sit back and reflect?"

Decision-making is compromised in another way. The shift in authority from cabinet ministers to the Prime Minister's Office (PMO) over the last thirty years is well documented. For prime ministers and their advisers, centralized control seems necessary to reduce mistakes by rookie ministers and maintain discipline in communications with an inattentive public. But centralization has costs. The burden on PMO staff is heavy, and the whole system is vulnerable to staffing problems at the centre. Cabinet's role as a deliberative body – never substantial – has shrunk. "Message discipline" means conformity and simplicity in talking points. There is less space for ambiguity and complexity, two essential features of any conversation about the future.

PLATFORM GOVERNANCE

Pressure of events is not the only thing that compromises the ability of leaders to look forward. Forward-thinking has also suffered because Canadian parties have changed their approach to governance. Platform governance, as I call it, encourages a focus on short-term electoral calculations and shifts responsibility for policy-making to political parties that are not equipped to perform that role competently. More fundamentally, it promotes an unrealistic view of what it means to govern.

Over the last two centuries, political scientists have defined the role of elected representatives in two ways. The first definition says that legislators act as trustees who exercise judgment about what is in the best interest of their constituents. The second definition says that legislators act as delegates who ask themselves what their constituents would want and act accordingly. A delegate would never consciously adopt a policy that is offensive to constituents, whereas trustees sometimes think they know better.

Obviously, the delegate model gives less discretion to legislators than the trustee model. But even delegates exercise discretion sometimes. Because events are unpredictable, legislators can never be sent to the national capital with complete instructions about what to do. When a new problem crops up, legislators have to decide whether it matters to their constituents, and they may have to go back and get fresh instructions on how to respond. In other words, serving as a delegate is still a dynamic and creative assignment.

There is a third model of representation that has become popular in Canada over the last thirty years, which limits the discretion of legislators even more stringently than the delegate model. Under this model, the critical players are parties, not legislators alone. Parties are hardly new, but their modus operandi has changed. Parties now behave like contractors providing services to blocs of voters. The party's campaign platform, which stipulates the services to be provided, forms the contract. Voters consent to the contract by electing a party into government. The party honours the contract by implementing promises made during the campaign. If a party fails to execute the contract, voters punish it at the next election.

A critical point is that parties, not individual members of Parliament, make promises to voter blocs. As a result, legislators do not have as much room to exercise discretion. Another critical point is that the platform model of governance does not allow for the unexpected. All the important things that a government must do while in office are specified in the platform. The possibility that legislators might have to return to their constituents for fresh instructions in the course of their service is not contemplated. So, the role of the legislator is limited here too.

Platforms are taken more seriously in Canada than they once were. The critical moment might have been the federal election of 1993, when the Liberal Party led by Jean Chrétien battled to replace the Progressive Conservative government led by Kim Campbell. Chrétien told his campaign team that he wanted "a detailed costed agenda for government … to which he would be held accountable four years later." The result was the 112-page Red Book, which was published by the party at the start of the election with the ceremony usually attached to government budget statements.

This was a significant change from the approach that Liberals had taken in earlier elections. Conventional wisdom in the 1970s and 1980s said that voters were swayed by factors like leadership or values rather than a party's stand on specific issues. In 1974, the Liberals won a majority with the slogan, "Issues Change from Year to Year: The Ability to Lead Does Not." This was the antithesis of platform governance. But the Red Book seemed to be the winning formula for Liberals in 1993, and the practice of publishing detailed manifestos became established. In 2006, Liberal adviser Eddie Goldenberg declared that parties had a duty to provide voters with "a detailed, well thought out, and carefully costed platform." He compared it to a five-year corporate plan.

Governmental institutions have been restructured to support platform governance. In 2017, federal law was amended so that an independent body, the Parliamentary Budget Office (PBO), had authority to estimate the cost of promises made by parties during campaigns. Journalists describe this as an "election platform costing service," even though the PBO itself says that it examines specific proposals rather than entire platforms. While parties are not required to request estimates from PBO, the mere existence of the procedure reinforces the notion that parties ought to have detailed and accurately costed platforms. During the 2019 and 2021 elections all major parties used the service, "suggesting that there was a strong incentive ... to take part."

Platform governance has been institutionalized in other ways. Since the 1970s, prime ministers have given instructions to new ministers in mandate letters. After the 1990s, these letters became more detailed, as prime ministers assigned responsibility for fulfilling promises contained in platforms. By 2013, mandate letters were "more important than ever." In 2015, the Trudeau government began publishing mandate letters, making ministers publicly accountable for their allotment of campaign promises. Today, publication of mandate letters has become the norm. In the fall of 2023, Trudeau was criticized for failing to publish fresh mandate letters within two months of a Cabinet shuffle.

In 2015, the Trudeau government also established a new office at the centre of government, and appointed "results officers" in each department, to monitor progress on its platform commitments. At the same time, it created a website, the Mandate Letter Tracker, so the public could keep score as well. A non-governmental group set up its own scorecard and concluded in 2019 that the Trudeau government had achieved 50 per cent of its promises in full, 40 per cent in part, and 10 per cent not at all.

The Trudeau government's enthusiasm for mandate tracking waned over the years, but the mentality of platform governance persists. Parties are expected to campaign for office based on platforms that are detailed and fully costed. During campaigns, platforms are graded for thoroughness and rigour. The duty of parties that win power is conceived as delivering on their platform commitments. Michael Barber, an adviser to the Trudeau government, said that governing was mainly about "the science of delivery," which he called deliverology. According to this theory, citizens hold governments accountable by keeping score of how many promises are actually fulfilled.

How exactly do parties formulate their platforms? This is left largely to the discretion of party leaders. Although parties periodically bring their members together for "policy conventions," the decisions taken at these meetings have no direct connection to the campaign platform. Resolutions approved at these conventions, says Paul Wells, "are just a chance for the rank-and-file membership to build pillow forts in the basement."

Sometimes, leaders have undertaken consultations with party members, legislators, and cabinet ministers while drafting the campaign platform. More often, though, critical decisions about the party platform are made by the party leader and a small number of advisers – political strategists, pollsters, and communications specialists – based on calculations about what is likely to appeal to key segments of the electorate. If the party is in government, even senior cabinet ministers may find that their role in preparing platforms is negligible.

In September 2023, a former adviser to Stephen Harper described the essence of platform governance. The Conservative policy convention held in Quebec City that month was really not about policymaking at all, said Yaroslav Baran. The convention was mainly a communications exercise; the campaign platform would be eventually drafted by the party leader and a small inner group. "Party leaders appoint platform teams," Baran explained. "Platform teams beget platforms; platforms beget Throne Speeches, and Throne Speeches beget ministerial mandate letters that set a new government's agenda."

Platform governance encourages a focus on the short term. Parties make promises that can be fulfilled quickly, so that points can be racked up on the scorecard before the next election. Parties also have incentives to make a lot of promises, micro-targeting many small blocs of swing voters. The Liberal platform of 2015 contained more than three hundred commitments. The mentality of platform governance drives party leaders toward shopping lists, not broad visions about grand strategy.

Platform governance can result in policy commitments that are poorly conceived or unworkable. Parties are pushed to make "firm and detailed policy decisions sooner rather than later" – that is, during the campaign and before a new government is sworn into office. But Canadian political parties have little capacity to think deeply about policy. A 2021 study found that there was no federal party in which senior officials considered policy formation to be a priority in the central party office. Party leaders in the House of Commons are allocated research staff, but these are mainly focused on public relations work or gathering incriminating information about political opponents.

Platform governance also limits the ability of public servants to provide advice about the workability of proposed policies. Officials cannot play a direct role in drafting party platforms because that would violate the principle of bureaucratic neutrality. Officials can only provide advice once a party has gained office. By then, though, it may be too late. Parties may have made promises based on incomplete information or ignorance of legal or bureaucratic constraints. Goldenberg acknowledged in 2006 that some platform commitments "are invariably later found to be unworkable." Tyler Meredith, a former adviser to Justin Trudeau, has agreed with Goldenberg. "There are some things where you learn more once you are in government," he said in 2023. "There may be a span of information that you didn't have access to, as to why it would be better to do something differently, or not to do something at all."

A more fundamental problem with platform governance is that it encourages a flawed view of what governance really requires. In the abstract, politicians acknowledge that politics is unpredictable and that dangers can arise suddenly from many directions. They like to quote former British prime minister Harold Macmillan, who suggested that politics was largely about responding to events. But platform governance is built on a model of the world in which events never intrude.

Platforms produced by the Chrétien government did not anticipate the economic crisis of 1994, the Quebec referendum crisis of 1995, or the terrorism crisis of 2001. The Conservative platform of 2008 did not account for the global economic crisis that was unfolding even as it was published. The Liberal platform of 2015 did not anticipate the election of Donald Trump in 2016 and its consequences for Canadian trade and industrial policy. The Liberal platform of 2019 did not anticipate the COVID pandemic of 2020, and its platform of 2021 did not anticipate the Freedom Convoy, war in Ukraine, and inflation in 2022.

"When we have elections we talk about things in very static terms," government house leader Mark Holland conceded in 2023, looking back on the 2019 and 2021 elections. "No one could have imagined a global pandemic. No one could have imagined a war in Ukraine. No one could have imagined what's happening with global inflation." Holland's statement is wrong on two levels. In fact, some experts warned specifically about these three dangers. More broadly, any realist would have anticipated some kind of disruption in 2022 and 2023, if not these specific crises. Realists assume that the world is turbulent and dangerous. Practitioners of platform governance believe that it is safe and predictable.

A defence of platform governance is that it has worked for political parties. Over the last thirty years, parties with well-crafted platforms have overcome voter distrust and won elections. But there is reason to wonder about the long-term effects of platform governance even for parties themselves. Parties may be winning elections in the short term by depleting their own credibility in the long run. A 2023 Proof Strategies poll found that public attitudes about parties are now highly unfavourable. Sixty per cent of Canadians saw parties as a "divisive force," bent mainly on gaining "just enough seats to advance their agenda," rather than bringing people together and unifying the country. Fewer than 20 per cent thought that parties aim to "discuss issues and bring people together." Canadians held these views regardless of their party affiliation.

DISINVESTING IN FORWARD-THINKING

Adaptability requires that decision-makers take a long and broad view of challenges that Canada will likely face, but the conditions of twenty-first-century politics make it harder than ever for leaders to do this. Time is short, pressure is intense, and electoral competition is fierce.

One remedy for this problem is to create and support organizations that can act as a counterweight to short-sightedness. But federal governments have gone the other way over the last thirty years, by reducing the capacity of public institutions to engage in forward-thinking. Non-governmental organizations are unable to make up for these cuts.

One possible check on short-sightedness is the federal bureaucracy itself. But the capacity of public servants to perform this role is limited even at the best of times. The public service only has as much room for forward-thinking as the government of the day allows it. Since the 1980s, Conservative and Liberal governments have been more reluctant to take policy advice from the bureaucracy, and during moments of austerity, they have cut the number of workers responsible for producing advice. Officials are expected to focus on delivery of platform commitments and on compliance with a growing number of controls and reporting requirements.

The limitations of the public service as a check against short-sightedness are illustrated by the history of the Policy Research Initiative. In 1995, responding to deep budget cuts over the previous two years, the Privy Council Office (PCO) commissioned a report on the state of policy capacity, defined as "the intellectual capacity to foresee problems and develop solutions for them," in federal departments. The Fellegi report, published in 1996, found that many departments, short-staffed and preoccupied with immediate problems, were neglecting longer-term policy work. The report concluded that the "central strategic problem" for federal government was its limited ability to "look over the horizon to identify new issues and position the government to deal with emerging trends or possible major developments." It recommended that PCO take the lead in promoting attention to longer-term issues.

The PCO responded by launching a project that came to be known as the Policy Research Initiative. A team of analysts within PCO worked with departments to produce research and develop networks with analysts outside government. Senior officials met regularly to discuss the work being done by these networks. Overall, policy capacity across federal government improved in the early 2000s. Still, the initiative's work had a limited effect on ministers who were preoccupied with immediate political problems in the final years of Liberal government.

The initiative's fortunes declined further after the election of the Harper government in 2006. The Policy Research Initiative was downgraded and moved out of PCO, and a new round of budget cuts once again led to reduced policy capacity across government. A 2015 study of policy capacity within the federal government echoed concerns that had been expressed by the Fellegi report twenty years earlier. Since 2015, the Trudeau government has taken steps to improve policy analysis capabilities but has not revived anything like the Policy Research Initiative within PCO itself.

Between the 1960s and 1980s, Ottawa tried to bolster its capacity for big thinking another way, by creating independent advisory councils. I described some of the most important councils in chapter 2. Many were eliminated after the 1980s. The death blow for some came in the 1992 budget of the Mulroney government. Aiming to make government "streamlined and less wasteful," Finance Minister Don Mazankowski announced the closing of the Economic Council of Canada, the Science Council of Canada, the Law Reform Commission of Canada, the Canadian Environmental Advisory Council, and several other advisory bodies. The savings were negligible, about $20 million a year. Some suspected that expense was not really the issue and that Conservative ministers were frustrated by council reports that clashed with government priorities.

While the cuts did little to reduce the federal deficit, they did have the effect of staunching conversation about national policy. Political scientist John Trent said at the time that the Mulroney government was "blindsiding the Canadian polity for decades." The president of the Canadian Chamber of Commerce, Tim Reid, said that government was shuttering bodies that were "important to the country's future prosperity." Nobel Laureate John Polanyi said that the government was "shooting itself in the head" by eliminating the science council. Another scholar said that eliminating the environmental council was "like gouging out your eyes" given the growing importance of environmental issues.

More advisory councils were eliminated in following years. The Chrétien government abolished the Canadian Advisory Council on the Status of Women in 1995 as part of its deficit-control program. The Law Reform Commission was revived in 1996 but eliminated again by the Harper government in 2006. (It was revived a second time, in modified form, in 2023.) Over the next six years, the Harper government closed the National Council of Welfare, which had been established in 1969, and three other bodies that focused on international relations and development.

Another tool for forward-thinking, the royal commission, has also been abandoned. Federal governments still appoint commissions of inquiry that are mainly concerned with exposing and correcting past wrongs, like the Gomery inquiry, which examined corruption in sponsorship and advertising programs; the 2016–19 inquiry into missing and murdered Indigenous women and girls; and the Truth and Reconciliation Commission, which exposed the history of residential schools. But the second type of commission, which is mainly prospective and promotes research and discussion about national challenges, has fallen into disuse. There have been only two in the last quarter-century: the 2001–02 Romanow Commission on health care and a 2009–12 inquiry on the decline of Fraser River salmon stocks. The days of the forward-looking royal commission, professor Evert Lindquist has observed, are "long gone."

There is no shortage of subjects that might be assigned to commissions. Former finance minister Bill Morneau said that he came into office in 2015 wanting to establish a royal commission on the tax system, modelled on the influential Carter Commission of the 1960s. "It was clear," Morneau said, "that a complete rethink of our system" was necessary, and a commission seemed to him to be the best way to do that. Later, academics Richard Nimijean and David Carment argued for a reprise of the Macdonald Commission of 1982–85, looking at Canada's economic and security challenges. In 2021, a dozen senators called for a reprise of the Massey Commission of 1949–51, to consider how cultural policy should be fitted to the realities of this century. In 2022, former senator Hugh Segal proposed a royal commission to draw lessons from the pandemic, while professor Donald Savoie proposed a reprise of the Glassco Commission of 1960–63, to examine how the federal public service might be improved. In 2023, former Liberal cabinet minister Sergio Marchi called for another royal commission on health care.

None of these proposals have been taken up. The basic premise of a royal commission – that leaders do not know what to do about a national challenge and ought to reflect on the subject – may be at odds with the ethos of platform governance, in which parties are expected to have precise ideas about how problems should be addressed.

Moreover, commissions are perceived as slow and risky. Morneau dispensed with the idea of a royal commission on taxation because the project could not be executed "within a four-year electoral calendar." He thought that the Liberal Party's capacity to control the agenda during the next campaign might be undermined if the commission was still working at that time. Added to this was the danger that a commission might make recommendations at odds with the government's own preferences.

As finance minister, Morneau turned to another device, popular in the Harper and Trudeau years: an external advisory committee, comprised of experts and notables working on a part-time and sometimes uncompensated basis, usually with a tight deadline. This promised to be a faster and less politically threatening way of acquiring advice. In 2020, Lisa Raitt, a former cabinet minister under Stephen Harper, explained the advantages of advisory committees: "One of the things that a politician will do is that they will set up advisory committees. You will consult wide and far in order to bring in the most pertinent information and the best experts to give you advice. Mind you, in the back room there's about fifteen officials and a secretariat who are actually drafting up what is going to be the position of the government going forward ... Not saying that your time isn't valuable as an outside expert, sometimes this stuff does work, but the reality is that a lot of this stuff has already been baked in."

Morneau's Advisory Council on Economic Growth was established in 2016 and wrapped up its work the following year. It was chaired by

Dominic Barton, a senior executive at the consulting firm McKinsey & Company. Morneau later lamented that the council's work had little impact on government policy or public opinion. But this was the inevitable result of how the council was organized. Real impact would have required an inquiry that had more independence, time, and resources.

CIVIL SOCIETY CANNOT FILL THE GAP

Successive governments have reduced their investment in institutions that specialize in forward-thinking. Sometimes this has been justified with the argument that there are more people and organizations outside government doing the same kind of work. But this is not true. Civil society, as academics call it, lacks the resources and status needed to replicate the work once done by independent councils and royal commissions.

It is certainly true that there are many more professors at Canadian universities who are producing high-quality research than there were thirty years ago. But university professors have a lot of freedom to decide what subjects they will explore. There is no guarantee that they will conduct research on pressing national questions or that they will all work together to do this research in a coordinated way. Moreover, professors are usually discouraged from doing speculative work about the future, and it is not part of their job description to promote public conversation about the work they do.

The number of special interest groups and government relations firms working in Ottawa has increased as well. Seven thousand people were registered as active lobbyists in Ottawa in 2022. But interest groups typically have little or no capacity for research, and the research that they do is tailored to the needs of their members. Similarly, government relations firms are not hired by businesses and interest groups with the aim of promoting balanced public discussion about long-run challenges. More often their aim is to secure financial advantages for their clients. Nor do these lobbyists claim any competence in policy research. A 2020 study found that "connections are more important than expertise" in Canada's government relations industry.

Canada has about one hundred think-tanks (non-profit organizations that conduct research and advocacy on policy questions), which is considerably more than it had forty years ago. But the capacity of Canadian think-tanks is limited. "All think tank leaders," an expert on Canadian think-tanks has observed, "believe their organizations to be precarious and lonely beacons." Almost always, they are right. Think-tanks in Canada scramble incessantly for philanthropic support, contracts to provide services for governmental or private clients, and media attention. A 2018 study found that only fifteen of the roughly one hundred Canadian think-tanks employed more than ten people, and only a few of this number are engaged in research. A single Washington think-tank, the Brookings Institution, had more revenue in 2018 than all major Canadian think-tanks combined. There have been some instances in which Canadian think-tanks have had a significant influence on government policy. On the whole, though, their impact on policy and public discussion in Canada has been modest.

The twenty-first century has also been a boomtime for social movements, as the Rouleau inquiry observed in 2023. Citizens can mobilize more quickly and sometimes raise large amounts of money. More than $20 million was collected for the 2022 Freedom Convoy, although much of this money was never used by organizers. By comparison, the Institute for Research on Public Policy, one of Canada's most respected think-tanks, had a budget of only $3 million in 2022.

But Internet-powered social movements tend to be ephemeral: they can dissolve as quickly as they emerge. Rarely do they have the capacity to raise large funds on a continuing basis. And movement organizers often oppose the very idea of hiring professional staff or supporting research rather than direct action because these choices threaten to kill the spirit of the movement. Populist movements are especially hostile to expertise and government. Even if the Freedom Convoy had been able to keep its $20 million, that money would not have been spent on a large-scale study of national strategy.

There are several reasons why governments in Canada are sometimes better placed to promote forward-thinking than civil society. The most obvious advantage is the ability of governments to provide significant funding on a steady basis. There are non-financial advantages too. Independent councils and royal commissions exercise a sort of gravitational force within the realm of public policy that cannot be replicated by non-governmental bodies. They draw collective attention to a problem and continue to do this in a sustained way over a period of years. This is another type of informal or soft coordination that helps to keep a loosely joined political system operating smoothly.

REINVESTING IN FORWARD-THINKING

What has happened in Ottawa over the past thirty years can be regarded as a story of adaptation. The conditions of politics have become more treacherous. In response to these new conditions, politicians have developed new techniques for acquiring public support for their parties and for the policies they adopt while in office. We could also view this as a story about the deepening of democracy in Canada. Citizens are more demanding, and politicians work harder to win their favour.

In some ways, the style of governance that has emerged in Canada is effective: parties have won power and the business of government has carried on. But innovations always have side effects, which become more obvious over time. Today, decision-makers in Ottawa have less time to think creatively. They are under more pressure to focus on the next election and are more prone to particularism, by which I mean the tendency to focus on actions that are likely to appeal to important slices of the electorate, rather than the public as a whole.

There is less incentive for leaders in Ottawa to promote research about national challenges because the results of that work may not be realized for years. There may even be political risks in doing this sort of work. In a world where attention is a scarce resource, focusing more on long-term challenges means focusing less on the government's short-term goals. Leaders have responded to these shifting incentives and risks by disinvesting in forward-thinking. The result is less research, conversation, and understanding about grand strategy.

A retreat from forward-thinking might not have seemed hazardous at the start of this century, when the entire world appeared to be approaching the end of history, a nirvana of stability, democracy, and self-regulating markets. Obviously, we are in a different world today, a more volatile world in which the course of history is harder to perceive. In this sort of world, we ought to be investing more, not less, in forward-thinking. In chapter 7, I explain how we can do this.

4

The Missing Dialogue

Canada is a federal state because its constitution distributes power among several parts – the federal government, provinces and territories, and Indigenous communities. This system has obvious advantages but also vulnerabilities. Adaptability is compromised if leaders disagree about dangers facing the country or address those dangers in contradictory ways. Obviously, complete agreement among leaders is unattainable. But there should be mechanisms to reduce dissonance so far as possible.

In twentieth-century Canada, one of those mechanisms was the first ministers' conference (FMC): a regular meeting, held with some degree of formality, that included the prime minister and provincial and territorial premiers. FMCs were a critical part of the system of intergovernmental diplomacy described by Richard Simeon in 1973. They were comparable to the international summit meetings that also became commonplace after World War II. There have been seventy-six FMCs since 1945, which averages to almost one a year.

Summits, including FMCs, may serve three purposes. One obvious goal is dealmaking: reaching a firm agreement on some question of policy. Less tangible but equally important is the goal of demonstrating solidarity. Leaders gather to show the world that they are committed

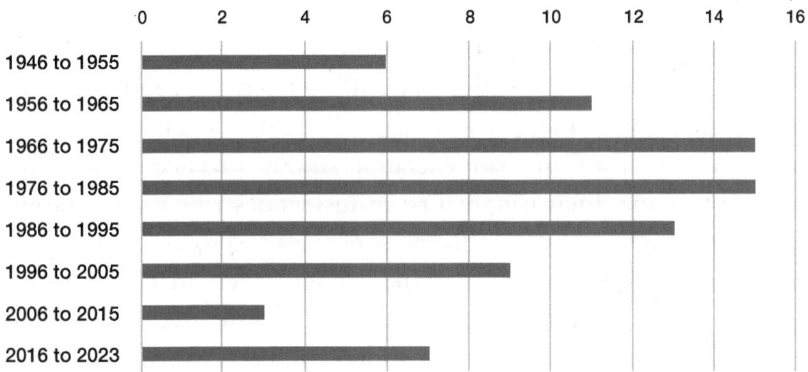

Figure 4.1 Number of first ministers' conferences, by decade from 1946 to 2023

to an alliance, even when they have sharp differences, and also to show they can talk civilly about those differences. The third purpose is deliberation: sharing information and points of view, to improve common understanding and promote coordinated action. In all three ways, summitry contributes to the adaptability of decentralized political systems.

Unfortunately, the FMC as an institution has broken down in Canada. As figure 4.1 shows, the one-a-year average since 1945 is misleading: FMCs have not been held regularly since the early 1990s. Since then, the norm of regular meetings has given way to a new norm, according to which FMCs are held at the discretion of the prime minister and avoided where possible. Prime ministers also have discretion about the form of FMCs, and meetings have become less formal and more one-sided. The most recent FMC, convened by Justin Trudeau in 2023, lasted barely two hours.

Federal policy about holding FMCs – or rather, not holding them – is increasingly idiosyncratic. Premiers themselves have headed in the opposite direction, by consolidating their practice of regular meetings. Leaders in other federal systems have done the same. And in the sphere of international relations, Canadian prime ministers are enthusiastic proponents of summitry. They tout the benefits of regular meetings with leaders from other countries, while denying that FMCs could produce the same benefits at home.

Canadian domestic summitry suffers from a second problem: marginalization of Indigenous leaders. There is a disconnect between rhetoric about the Canadian federation and the practice of summitry within Canada. Increasingly, first ministers describe the federation as a partnership between Indigenous peoples and federal, provincial, and territorial governments. But Indigenous leaders are not treated as partners when first ministers convene. First ministers retain discretion about when and how Indigenous leaders will participate.

Canadian prime ministers may have had good reasons for retreating from regular FMCs in the late 1990s. A respite from summitry seemed like a good way of restoring calm to national politics. But circumstances have changed dramatically since the 1990s. The Canadian political system has more moving parts, the world is more complicated, and antagonisms among Canadian leaders are festering. There is a greater need for leaders to show solidarity, talk through their differences, and seek a common understanding on national strategy. As Canadian leaders routinely acknowledge in other contexts, these are the benefits produced by well-designed summit meetings. Regular summits of Canadian leaders would help a loosely joined system to respond intelligently to emerging dangers.

THE RISE OF FIRST MINISTERS' MEETINGS

As I explained in chapter 2, Canada in the late twentieth century developed an elaborate system of intergovernmental relations that was designed to manage the vulnerabilities intrinsic to federal states. Civil servants in different governments established routines for sharing information, coordinating action, and resolving disputes.

Problems that could not be resolved by civil servants were pushed up to the ministers who headed their departments, and procedures for regular consultation among ministers were established as well. Provincial and federal finance ministers have met regularly since 1959, health ministers since 1960, environment ministers since 1964, education ministers since 1967, forest and fisheries ministers since the 1980s, immigration ministers since 2002, and Indigenous affairs ministers since 2016. Some of these ministerial groups have dedicated secretariats to support their work.

However, there are some problems that cannot be resolved with meetings of this type. Ministers can speak authoritatively on subjects falling within the remit of their department. They cannot engage on questions of grand strategy. Only first ministers can do this. For this reason, the FMC was placed at the apex of the system of intergovernmental coordination, to address the biggest and most difficult questions of national policy.

The first FMC was held in 1906, but the practice of holding regular meetings took root in the 1930s as leaders struggled for a response to the Great Depression. Six FMCs were held between 1931 and 1941. Their value was generally appreciated. In its 1939 report on the state of Canadian federalism, the Rowell-Sirois Commission said that the need for regular meetings was "obvious," adding that they "conduce to the more efficient working of the federal system." Another 1941 study said that it was "natural" for first ministers to meet regularly "to discuss conflicts between them and common problems, and perhaps devise common remedies for such difficulties."

After World War II, first ministers' meetings became commonplace as the leaders developed plans for expanding the welfare state, invented new methods of collecting and sharing taxes, and explored ways of reforming the constitution to fit a changing country. Twenty-five meetings were held between 1945 and 1970. One commentator observed in 1965 that the practice of regular FMCs was practically "built into Canada's constitution." The 1971 Victoria Charter, a bundle of constitutional reforms that was agreed upon by all governments except Quebec, would have made an annual meeting of first ministers a formal requirement.

Although the Victoria Charter was not adopted, the pace of FMCs did not slacken. There were thirty-one meetings between 1971 and 1992, dedicated not just to constitutional reform but also to the economic shocks of the 1970s and the project of economic liberalization that followed in the 1980s. In its 1979 report, the Pepin-Roberts Task Force on Canadian Unity said that recent meetings on economic strategy had shown "real promise" and that first ministers' conferences ought to be held on a "regular annual basis." Brian Mulroney, elected prime minister in 1984, promised to hold annual meetings on the economy, "to ensure a regular opportunity for consultation and coordination," and did so for the remainder of that decade.

By then, it was conventional wisdom that first ministers' meetings were "the principal forum for the conduct of intergovernmental business in Canada." In its 1985 report, the Macdonald Royal Commission on the Economic Union and Development Prospects for Canada said that there should be a constitutional requirement for annual first ministers' meetings, "to provide essential recognition of the need to manage intergovernmental interdependence, and the need to co-ordinate policies and activities." The Meech Lake Accord, a package of constitutional reforms prepared in 1987, included a commitment to meetings at least once a year. Another reform effort, the 1992 Charlottetown Accord, also included the promise of annual meetings.

THE DECLINE OF FIRST MINISTERS' MEETINGS

Neither the Meech Lake nor Charlottetown accord was adopted, but not because of controversy over the need for regular first ministers' meetings. This was a minor item. Still, the failure of these two constitutional reform projects had a profound effect on the attitude of prime ministers and their advisers toward FMCs. From the 1930s until the 1980s, the need for regular meetings was generally accepted. After the early 1990s, however, the discretionary principle began to take hold, as I suggested earlier. Meetings were held only when the prime minister thought them necessary and, if possible, not at all.

This shift came about for two reasons. FMCs had come to be regarded exclusively as vehicles as for dealmaking, mainly on the subject of constitutional reform. The other purposes of FMCs were overlooked. From the point of view of constitutional dealmaking, FMCs were not only demonstrably ineffectual but also procedurally flawed. The Canadian public recoiled at closed-door decision-making by first ministers on fundamental questions of regime design. More generally, Canadians in the early 1990s were exhausted by years of constitutional wrangling, and the reputation of first ministers' meetings suffered by association.

Jean Chrétien, prime minister after 1993, had a personal predisposition against FMCs. As a minister in the 1970s, Chrétien had objected to long-winded Cabinet discussions, and he felt the same way about FMCs. "Prolonged palavers" were not his style. And Chrétien judged that it was not prudent, given the delicate state of national politics in the early 1990s, to risk putting the country "through the wringer of any more failed conferences."

Chrétien's first two FMCs were convened only after the terms of new federal–provincial agreements had been hammered out by lower-level officials. The third was held because the 1982 constitution required it to review certain provisions of that document. And when an FMC seemed necessary in 2000 to address health care funding, Chrétien displayed his antipathy toward long conversations: "At the outset of the meeting … I informed the premiers that the game was over: what was on the table was all they would be getting, and Ottawa wanted something back … When six of the premiers unexpectedly objected … I got up and walked out of the room … Once I had cooled down sufficiently, I returned, but only to deliver a short, clear message: no conditions, no money. Then I left again … [The premiers] soon broke down and grabbed the money."

The need for FMCs also seemed to dissipate because of another shift in the dynamics in federal–provincial relations in the 1990s. The Chrétien government spent much of the decade responding to secessionist pressures in Quebec, and it did this in part by negotiating special arrangements that allowed Quebec more autonomy in areas such as immigration, job training, and health care. Other provinces soon asked for similar treatment. National agreements settled in the context of first ministers' conferences were displaced by bilateral agreements negotiated between Ottawa and each province. Constitutional expert Peter Russell thought that the country was shifting to a new form of "make-a-deal federalism." This style of governing had the advantage of reducing the temperature of national politics. It also allowed Ottawa to gain an upper hand by applying a strategy of divide-and-conquer among the provinces.

In the late 1980s, first ministers' meetings had been seen as "a core institutional feature of Canadian federalism." Fifteen years later, this was no longer true. In 2004, Martin Papillon and Richard Simeon observed that first ministers' meetings were "ad hoc and sporadic" events, "often motivated by political ends only remotely tied to the management of interdependence between two orders of government."

There was a brief resurgence of FMC activity in 2004. Prime Minister Paul Martin called three meetings in one year, in a vain effort to demonstrate the vigour of his short-lived government by negotiating grand agreements on federal–provincial financing and Indigenous affairs. This did little to counter suspicions that FMCs were mainly vehicles for advancing the political ambitions of the prime minister.

The significance of first ministers' meetings plummeted even further after the election of the Conservative government in 2006. Prime Minister Stephen Harper promised during the 2006 campaign that he would work closely with provinces to "strengthen intergovernmental cooperation." But Harper's predisposition was that the roles of federal and provincial governments should be demarcated more sharply and that Ottawa's role in national affairs ought to be limited. If these changes were made, it followed in Harper's mind that there was less need for first ministers' meetings.

Senior federal officials, including the outgoing head of the public service, Alex Himelfarb, also discouraged Harper from holding FMCs as Martin did. "Alex could just barely contain himself with the 'Don't ever do this,'" one of Harper's former aides told journalist Paul Wells. But there was little danger that Harper would do otherwise. He shared Chrétien's distaste for high-profile sessions with premiers. "The grand gesture of a conference of first ministers," John Ibbitson wrote in 2015, "is a gesture that he prefers to avoid."

Harper met premiers only four times in almost ten years. The first meeting was an informal dinner in 2006 with no agenda for discussion. There was another dinner meeting in January 2008. As the global financial crisis intensified that year, Harper felt pressure to meet again, for one afternoon in November 2008. Harper described it as "a very preliminary discussion on a wide range of issues." In 2009, as the global economy moved into its deepest slump since World War II, Harper finally convened a formal, full-day meeting of first ministers.

By the end of Harper's first government, the discretionary principle regarding FMCs had taken complete hold. As an official explained in 2011, FMCs were "called at the whim of the PM." Harper never convened another meeting during his remaining five years as prime minister. He preferred to deal one-on-one with premiers. Harper's office claimed in 2012 that he had more than 250 one-on-one meetings with premiers in his first six years in office. Often these were followed by agreements with individual provinces. "Bilateralism," Christopher Dunn observed at the end of Harper's tenure, "was the dominant mode for relations with other ministers." Even these bilateral relationships could be fraught. Harper met with Ontario premier Kathleen Wynne only once in his last two years in office.

Some observers claimed that Harper's approach to federal–provincial relations was good for the country. Ibbitson credited Harper for giving Canada "something it hadn't experienced since the 1950s: quiet." The result, Ibbitson said, was that Canadians were more united than they had ever been in modern history. However, critics wondered whether Harper's approach had also compromised the country's ability to look forward. "His eschewing of First Ministers' Meetings," Jennifer Ditchburn and Graham Fox said, might have "weakened our ability to forge a national consensus on important issues and coordinate policy responses from coast to coast to coast."

During the 2015 election, Justin Trudeau promised that his government would "hold a first ministers' conference every single year." Trudeau has not delivered on this promise. He has called more meetings than Harper, but the principle of an annual meeting has not been established. Trudeau convened first ministers' meetings in 2015 and 2017 because he thought them necessary to move forward on one of the federal government's top priorities, climate change legislation. And first ministers spoke regularly by phone or videoconference during the COVID emergency of 2020–21. In general, though, the Trudeau government refused to surrender discretion in deciding whether a meeting would be held, how it would be organized, and what would be discussed. On important issues like health care and child care, it preferred to work bilaterally with individual provinces, just as the Harper government had done.

Michael Wernick, head of the public service for three years of the Trudeau government, restated the discretionary principle in a 2021 book. Wernick warned future prime ministers that they will "run into the temptation to convene a meeting of first ministers from time to time." The temptation should be resisted, Wernick said. Prime ministers should only hold meetings of first ministers when it suits their interest: to give profile to some issue that matters to the federal government, complete the formalities of an agreement with premiers, or manage a national emergency. Otherwise, "it is rarely to your advantage to get together with the premiers as a group … The federation works just fine without your personal involvement or a lot of meetings of first ministers."

The Trudeau government's approach to FMCs was illustrated in early 2023. First ministers might have convened in person in 2022, but they did not, despite Trudeau's promise of meetings every year. In July 2022, as pressures on provincial health care systems intensified, premiers joined in an "urgent call" for a first ministers' meeting to discuss federal contributions toward health care financing. Trudeau refused to convene a meeting until the fundamentals of a deal on federal funding were settled. In February 2023, Trudeau relented.

This meeting did not amount to much. It was preceded by a photo opportunity between Trudeau and Alberta premier Danielle Smith in which the two leaders struggled to shake hands properly. During the meeting itself, Trudeau presented the federal offer on health care financing and made clear that it was non-negotiable, much as Chrétien had done in 2000. The details "came fast and furious," Northwest Territories premier Caroline Cochrane said, so fast that it was difficult to comprehend them. And then the meeting was over. It had been shorter than an Air Canada flight from Ottawa to Winnipeg. There was no other meeting of first ministers in the remainder of 2023.

SUMMITRY AMONG PROVINCES AND TERRITORIES

When a practice becomes established as a norm and is conducted according to generally accepted routines, it is said to be institutionalized. When norms and routines fade away, the practice is deinstitutionalized. FMCs were institutionalized in Canada between the 1930s and 1980s and then deinstitutionalized after the 1990s.

Oddly, though, relationships among premiers alone have evolved in the opposite direction. Interprovincial relations have become more deeply institutionalized. Premiers never ask: should we meet this year? Meetings are part of the routine of governance.

Premiers of the three Prairie provinces constituted themselves as the Prairie Economic Council and began meeting annually in 1965. In 1973, British Columbia joined the group, which then met regularly as the Western Premiers' Conference. In the 1990s, the three northern territories were added. The annual conference of the seven leaders provides "an important opportunity to discuss shared priorities," Yukon premier Sandy Silver explained in 2022.

Premiers of the three Maritime provinces have been meeting regularly since the early 1970s. The Council of Maritime Premiers was set up in 1971 "to promote unity of purpose among the three provincial governments ... [and] establish the framework for joint action." The council was given its own secretariat to organize meetings and conduct research. In 2000, the body was reconfigured as the Council of Atlantic Premiers, now including Newfoundland. The four premiers agreed to meet at least twice a year, and more often if necessary.

All of Canada's premiers began meeting annually in 1960. By the 1990s, the Annual Premiers' Conference had developed into "a significant intergovernmental institution ... professionally supported by provincial civil servants." In 2003, premiers went a step further by establishing the Council of the Federation, with its own secretariat based in Ottawa. Premiers take turns chairing the council, which meets annually to discuss an agenda that is jointly determined.

Premiers did not invent the title of their new organization. The 1979 Task Force on Canadian Unity had proposed a Council of the Federation, configured differently and with law-making powers. In 1991 the Mulroney government also proposed a Council of the Federation, consisting of all first ministers, again with law-making power.

The council that was actually established in 2003 had no authority to make laws. It is a purely deliberative body. Moreover, it does not include the prime minister. Some premiers wanted to exclude the federal government because they saw the council as a vehicle for building a common front against Ottawa. "It is important the provinces and territories be united," Quebec premier François Legault explained in 2022, "and that we speak in one, single, united voice." Sometimes this means speaking with a united voice to demand a meeting with the prime minister, as premiers did in late 2022.

Premiers are driven to make united calls for FMCs because prime ministers are hesitant to convene meetings except in extraordinary circumstances. Prime ministers justify their hesitancy by arguing that regular meetings would be fruitless, given the oppositional mentality of premiers, illustrated by their habit of making united demands for meetings with the prime minister. The two levels of government seem to be caught in a vicious circle.

In any event, exclusion of the federal government from the council means that the body is mislabelled. It is a council of provinces and territories, not a council of the federation. It has been established because premiers recognized that regular meetings served the three important purposes that I identified at the start of this chapter: demonstrating solidarity, deliberating about shared priorities, and occasionally dealmaking.

SUMMITRY AMONG NATIONS

Summitry has become more institutionalized in the realm of international relations as well. While Canadian prime ministers question the value of regular FMCs, they enthuse about their meetings with heads of government from other countries.

In this respect, Justin Trudeau is no different from his predecessors. Trudeau has attended G7 summits every year since 2016, except for 2020, when the meeting was cancelled because of the COVID pandemic. Similarly, he has attended annual meetings of G20 leaders, APEC leaders, and NATO leaders, as well as annual gatherings of the United Nations General Assembly. He has attended biennial meetings of leaders from Commonwealth countries and La Francophonie, and the triennial Summit of the Americas. All this is done as a matter of routine. No one asks whether regular meetings are strictly necessary.

Leaders of the G7 countries, a set of affluent democracies, have met annually for a half-century. Meetings continue because the need to convene regularly seems obvious to everyone involved. The multiple purposes of summitry are routinely invoked. The G7 meeting demonstrates solidarity among "like-minded countries who are committed to democracy." It allows these countries to "govern together." It provides an opportunity for leaders to "discuss major, often complex international issues, and to develop the personal relationships that help them respond in effective collective fashion to sudden crises or shocks."

The Canadian government is deeply invested in the practice of holding G7 meetings. It hosted the 2010 summit at a cost of $300 million. Stephen Harper rebuffed complaints about the cost, insisting that the G7 was "a pretty essential organization going forward." When Canada hosted the summit again in 2018, the cost had doubled to $600 million. Still, Justin Trudeau defended the meeting as "an important opportunity to take concerted action on the world's most pressing challenges."

The summit will be held in Canada again in 2025. The Trudeau government says that the meeting will allow "frank and open discussion between leaders … on pervasive and crosscutting issues." It also says that the G7 summit provides a valuable focal point for civil society organizations, which often hold their own summits to prepare recommendations for G7 leaders. The same arguments could be made to justify regular meetings of Canadian leaders.

SUMMITRY WITHIN OTHER FEDERAL SYSTEMS

While deinstitutionalized in Canada, summitry among first ministers has been institutionalized in other federal systems. Australia, like Canada, experienced a crisis of intergovernmental relations in the early 1990s. But events took a different course afterward. While Canada retreated from FMCs, Australia's crisis led to creation of the Council of Australian Governments, which pledged to hold meetings of all national leaders at least once a year to promote "cooperation in the national interest."

Ironically, one influence on Australian policy-makers was Canada's Rowell-Sirois Commission, which recommended regular meetings in its 1939 report. By 2020, the Australian council had met almost fifty times. A second crisis, the COVID pandemic of 2020–21, led to the transformation of the council into the National Cabinet, with a commitment to monthly meetings among first ministers.

In India, first ministers have met regularly since 1950. Until 2015, they convened as the National Development Council, which oversaw the country's powerful Planning Commission. The council reviewed plans that were prepared by the commission and guided budget decisions. Advocates of central planning saw the council as a device for producing national development strategies that had the support of central and state governments.

Enthusiasm for central planning died in the 1990s, and in 2015 the commission was replaced by NITI Aayog, which functions as a think-tank rather than a spending body. NITI Aayog is overseen by a Governance Council that meets annually and includes all first ministers. The new council's role is to "evolve a shared vision of national development priorities," supported by research done by NITI Aayog. The new arrangement is not perfect. In 2022, one state leader boycotted the annual meeting, protesting that central government was manipulating the agenda and ignoring the opinions of state leaders. Many critics think that NITI Aayog should do more by reclaiming powers of the Planning Commission. But few advocate for it doing less.

Leaders also meet regularly within the European Union, another complex federal system. The European Council includes heads of government for the twenty-seven countries that constitute the union, as well as leaders of EU institutions in Brussels. Since 2007, the European Council has been formally recognized in the EU constitution. But this was not always the case. For more than thirty years, the council operated as an informal body, invented to remedy a serious flaw in the original approach to European integration.

When European governments began merging activities within the new European Economic Community in the 1950s, there was no plan for national leaders to meet regularly. The expectation was that coordination between governments would be handled by bureaucrats and sometimes ministers, just as in Canada today. But it became "increasingly obvious that the [European Economic Community] had no clear sense of direction." European leaders recognized the need for some process to establish long-term goals for the community.

The solution was summitry. European leaders met sporadically in the 1960s and early 1970s and agreed in 1974 to convene regularly as the European Council. The council met at least twice a year for the next three decades. The EU constitution now affirms the council's role in setting "general political directions and priorities" for the union and requires that it meet four times a year. The council has proved useful in formulating coordinated responses to crises such as the COVID pandemic and the war in Ukraine. One observer describes the council as a "political power station" that channels energy from each member country into projects that benefit the EU as a whole.

EXCLUSION OF INDIGENOUS LEADERS

Governance in Canada is compromised by the lack of regular FMCs. And there is a further difficulty, as mentioned earlier. Even when meetings are held, Indigenous leaders may not be allowed to participate. The same holds true when premiers alone meet. First ministers reserve discretion to decide when and how Indigenous leaders will participate in conversation about national challenges. This is not consistent with the claim that Indigenous peoples are partners in the Canadian federation.

There was a time in Canadian history when the idea of Indigenous representation in a summit of Canadian leaders would have seemed absurd. In the 1950s, Indigenous peoples were treated as political nonentities. The standard textbook on Canadian government at that time, written by Robert MacGregor Dawson, acknowledged that most Indigenous people could not vote. Nevertheless, Dawson insisted that Canada had "full adult suffrage" because he perceived self-government as a prerogative of the settler population alone. The idea of federalism, as Dawson called it, meant that authority on Canadian territory was distributed exclusively between federal and provincial governments. Indigenous societies on Canadian territory had no right of self-government, and the Canadian state had no significant obligations toward any of these societies.

Attitudes had shifted only slightly by the end of the 1960s. Indigenous peoples were allowed to vote in federal and provincial elections, but self-rule was still denied to Indigenous societies. The 1970 edition of Dawson's textbook explained that federal and provincial power was "unfettered by Indian treaties." An infamous 1969 discussion paper issued by the Pierre Trudeau government said that Indigenous peoples should have exactly the same rights and obligations as other Canadians, no more or less. Any treaties with Indigenous peoples contained "limited and minimal promises" that governments had largely fulfilled.

In the last decades of the twentieth century, understandings about the rights of Indigenous peoples were transformed. The principle that Indigenous peoples have sovereignty rights, sometimes modulated by treaties with settler governments, is now generally accepted. Canadians have acknowledged that settler governments ignored treaty obligations and tried to destroy Indigenous societies and that reparation for these harms is past due.

Policy-makers and scholars have struggled to find a simple way of describing an idea of federalism that accommodates Indigenous peoples. The 1996 Royal Commission on Aboriginal Peoples suggested that Indigenous governments should be recognized as a "third order" in the federation, alongside federal and provincial governments. Others have imagined the Canadian state as a composite of two federations – one comprised of federal and provincial governments, the other constituted by treaty relations between the Canadian state and Indigenous nations. Indigenous governments have also been envisaged as equal actors within a system of "multi-level governance."

Consensus on the best formulation is unlikely to emerge soon. But one point is clear: Dawson's idea of federalism, recognizing only federal and provincial governments, is obsolete. In whatever way the idea of federalism may be reformulated, Indigenous peoples ought to be treated as "full partners in Confederation," as the Truth and Reconciliation Commission said in 2015.

But Indigenous leaders are not treated as full partners when FMCs are convened. There were no representatives of Indigenous peoples at the table when first ministers met in 1981 to negotiate about patriation of the Constitution, although they did attend a series of meetings on Indigenous issues later in the 1980s. Indigenous representatives were absent again when first ministers met to discuss constitutional reform in 1987. This absence proved fatal for the Meech Lake Accord when Manitoba MLA Elijah Harper prevented the Manitoba legislature from ratifying the accord for this reason. When first ministers reconvened to negotiate the Charlottetown Accord in 1992, leaders of national Indigenous organizations were included in the discussions.

Indigenous leaders believe that the Charlottetown negotiations affirmed a qualified right of attendance at FMCs. When fundamental constitutional reforms are discussed, they will be guaranteed seats at the table, rather than being treated "indirectly as supplicants." The principle of "automatic inclusion" also seems to apply when first ministers deal with issues that directly affect Indigenous peoples, even if constitutional questions are not involved. Five national Indigenous organizations participated in the 2004 first ministers' meeting that produced the Kelowna Accord on social policy for Indigenous peoples. That accord included a promise of more meetings between first ministers and Indigenous leaders. But the accord was rejected by incoming prime minister Stephen Harper, and Indigenous leaders were not invited to join a first ministers' meeting for another fourteen years, when Justin Trudeau convened a conference to discuss economic development within Indigenous communities.

The standing of national Indigenous organizations is more ambiguous when a first ministers' meeting is not directly focused on Indigenous affairs. Indigenous leaders asked for an invitation when Prime Minister Jean Chrétien gathered premiers in 1997 to discuss a new framework for the evolution of social policy in Canada, but Chrétien's staff "shrugged off the request." Indigenous organizations were "excluded ... from any meaningful role" in developing the new framework. According to Christopher Alcantara and Jen Nelles, the 1997 meeting demonstrated that the inclusion of Indigenous leaders ultimately "depends on whether the prime minister feels that the agenda requires [it]." This is a restatement of the discretionary principle: when and how FMCs should be organized are questions to be settled by the prime minister alone.

The discretionary principle was at work again in 2023 when Justin Trudeau convened a meeting of first ministers on health care financing. RoseAnne Archibald, grand chief of the Assembly of First Nations, asked for an invitation, saying that it was "imperative to ensuring First Nations are no longer an after-thought in Canada's health-care system." But no invitation was extended. Archibald complained that Indigenous leaders were again being told to "wait outside of rooms where we belong."

The relationship of Indigenous leaders to the Council of the Federation is scarcely more satisfactory. The constitution of the council is a memorandum of understanding agreed to by premiers in 2003. It restates the idea of federalism described by Dawson forty years earlier. Indigenous peoples are not mentioned. Canada has "two orders of government," according to the memorandum, not three. The only "partners of the federation" envisaged in the memorandum are Ottawa and the provinces and territories.

In 2004, the council invited Indigenous leaders to meet with premiers before the annual summit of premiers themselves. The practice has continued even though it has frustrated Indigenous leaders, who complain that they attend "at the choice of the premiers, not out of obligation or necessity." Moreover, Indigenous leaders participate in a side meeting rather than the summit itself. In 2017 and 2018, several Indigenous organizations declined to meet with the premiers, complaining that the council was treating Indigenous peoples as "just another special interest group" rather than "nations with inherent rights." They relented and rejoined the meetings in 2019.

One reason that first ministers resist the routine inclusion of national Indigenous organizations is that they are not governments with authority to make binding agreements on behalf of Indigenous peoples. If summitry were only about dealmaking, this might be a decisive argument. But as I observed at the start of this chapter, summits serve symbolic and deliberative purposes too, and from this point of view the treatment of national Indigenous organizations is problematic. There is no place in which Indigenous leaders have a right to engage regularly with first ministers about the general affairs of the country. Participation always depends on the grace of the prime minister or premiers. "Indigenous organizations," Martin Papillon observed in 2020, "are still not full-fledged partners in the machinery of executive federalism."

BRINGING SUMMITRY HOME

Summitry in Canada, as it has evolved over the last thirty years, is a confused business. The practice of annual premiers' conferences is now more deeply entrenched. Similarly, the practice of attending and hosting international summits is now more deeply entrenched. In both contexts, Canadian leaders acknowledge the many advantages of regular meetings: for demonstrating solidarity, deliberating about shared challenges, and periodically making deals.

But there is one critical way in which Canada has marched in the opposite direction. Canadian prime ministers have abandoned the tradition of regular FMCs. There is no assurance in any year that there will be a meeting of Canadian leaders, and when they do meet, there is no consistency in format. A meeting might simply be a dinner conversation or a briefing for premiers with no conversation afterward. There is no process for agreeing on an agenda. Indigenous leaders may or may not be present. Prime ministers have discretion over the details and generally prefer not to meet at all.

In the 1990s, a retreat from the practice of holding regular FMCs might have made sense. Meetings became less frequent and less formal because it seemed to prime ministers and their advisers that they were doing more harm than good. Perhaps they were right. It is probable, though, that prime ministers dwelt too much on the difficulty of making deals within FMCs while neglecting the less tangible goals of demonstrating solidarity and deliberating about shared challenges.

In any case, conditions today are not what they were in the late 1990s. There are new threats to the Canadian union. The Canadian political system is more complex and decentralized than it was a generation ago, and centrifugal pressures within it are stronger. Public skepticism about the value of federalism is growing, particularly in the West. Provincial and territorial leaders, also struggling to retain power in the era of permanent campaigns, have powerful incentives to lobby against Ottawa. Antagonism between some first ministers is expressed openly. And the relatively benign policy environment of the late 1990s has disappeared. Disharmony and lack of coordination among governments may be more costly than it once was.

All of this argues for a revival of summitry in Canada. The logic that is applied in the sphere of international relations, and by leaders in other federations, and by premiers alone, ought to be applied to FMCs as well. A regular summit would demonstrate that Canadian leaders (first ministers and Indigenous representatives too) are allied in a common cause. It would promote shared understanding about long-term challenges. And it would demonstrate that civil discussion remains possible despite sharp differences of opinion. I elaborate on the details in chapter 7.

5

The Decaying Public Sphere

In chapter 2, I introduced the concept of the public sphere: a shared space in which citizens communicate with one another about problems facing their community and how to deal with them. The public sphere includes all the ways by which citizens talk about public affairs, from broadcast television to social media to neighbourhood meetings.

The concept may seem vague, but a healthy public sphere is an essential part of any democratic system. Imagine a system in which governments can communicate with citizens, but citizens cannot easily communicate with each other. (China, for example.) Maybe governments could retain the loyalty of citizens in such a system, but it would be difficult to say that citizens are in charge. A functioning democracy needs lines of communication among citizens so they can form a common understanding of problems and goals and collectively influence the direction of government action.

A healthy public sphere is also essential to adaptability. One of the main advantages of the Western model of governance – its ability to tap the creativity of people and groups outside government – can only be realized if the public sphere operates properly. As well as creativity, the public sphere generates legitimacy. That is, it deepens public understanding of what leaders are trying to do, so that citizens are less likely to resist government action, as many did during the COVID pandemic. The public sphere also promotes coordination of action within a highly decentralized system. If people have a common understanding of what the country is trying to accomplish, they are more likely to work in complementary rather than contradictory ways.

A healthy public sphere has four attributes. First, it has well-defined boundaries, so that all citizens are included, and citizens rather than non-citizens play the main role in steering discussion. Second, it has a reasonably stable agenda, so that people can predict what is likely to be discussed in the foreseeable future and prepare accordingly. Third, it has well-established norms about civility and open-mindedness in discourse. We talk and listen even when we disagree profoundly. And fourth, citizens are sufficiently well-informed that they can participate constructively in debate. They know about the history of their country, their system of government, and challenges ahead.

The existence of a healthy public sphere cannot be taken for granted. In any country, its existence depends on state action: through the provision of public education, support for communications infrastructure and media, guarantees of free speech, and other measures. In twentieth-century Canada, the fragility of the public sphere was a continuing preoccupation. Leaders understood that Canadian sovereignty meant nothing if Canadian citizens could not talk to one another constructively, and that their capacity to do this was compromised by a small population, vast geography, linguistic diversity, and foreign influences. Moreover, measures to protect the public sphere in Canada were constantly upended by technological change. Every advance in communication technologies was followed by a reappraisal of the measures necessary for preserving the public sphere, given the change in circumstances.

Canadians in 2024 are in a familiar position. Over the last thirty years, a series of technological shocks – such as the Internet, smartphones, social media, and related innovations – have upended the Canadian public sphere. Social networks have been rewired so that foreign corporations and groups wield more influence over the substance of debate in Canada. The agenda within the public sphere has been destabilized, so that Canadians who try to follow the national conversation are more easily exhausted and less likely to pay attention. Civility and rationality of debate have declined. And public understanding of national challenges has been compromised by a technology-driven crisis within Canadian journalism.

The problems facing the Canadian public sphere are not caused by technological shifts alone. The public sphere is also weakened because Canadians know too little about their history, their system of government, and the challenges that lie ahead. This is mainly a failure of government policy in the spheres of education and public affairs.

And there is a second and larger failure of government policy. Recent federal responses to technology shock have lacked coherence and broad political support. Some measures that the federal government has taken to protect the public sphere have been poorly designed and hotly contested. There appears to be no common understanding about the aims of national policy regarding the protection of democratic deliberation in Canada. This is partly because Canadian governments no longer think so carefully before they act, as I explained in chapter 3, and partly, perhaps, because decay of the public sphere has compromised the country's ability to think clearly about ways of preserving it.

ERODING BOUNDARIES OF THE PUBLIC SPHERE

A healthy public sphere is one in which Canadians rather than foreigners play the main role in setting the agenda and steering conversation. This problem of restraining foreign influences preoccupied policy-makers throughout the twentieth century. The problem has flared up again in the twenty-first century. One way to understand this is to consider how digital technologies have transformed the news business and how Canadians participate in politics.

In the 1980s, the newspaper industry was still a critical part of the Canadian public sphere. Newspapers were the main source of information about public affairs and one of the most important places where arguments about public policy were played out. Most Canadians read a newspaper every day. Newspapers were generally more trusted than radio or television news, and in any case, broadcasters usually followed the lead of newspapers. A handful of prestige newspapers and two national news services shaped coverage of public affairs across the country. The CBC, a federal corporation, was the dominant player in broadcast news.

Critics complained that the news business was slow, stuffy, and dominated by central Canadian elites. But the system had three virtues. First, it was nationally integrated, so that people in Newfoundland and British Columbia received similar packets of news. Second, news media were owned and operated by Canadians, largely because of federal government restrictions on foreign ownership. Third, the news agenda was fairly stable, in the sense that the list of major issues did not change as quickly as it does now. Political leaders were in a better position to guide that agenda than they are today. The conversation was well structured, although it skewed toward elite concerns.

The public sphere as it existed in the 1980s gave a restricted role to ordinary citizens. Print and broadcast news operated mainly in one direction. Citizens received news coverage, but they did not produce it, except perhaps by writing a letter to the editor. People engaged in other ways too: by talking about the news with friends and co-workers, contacting government officials, participating in party politics, voting, and persuading other people about their vote. Conversation was strongly guided by newspapers and broadcasters, and it was largely local. To put it roughly, Canadians talked to neighbours about what they read in the newspaper.

This world was disrupted by the advent of the Internet. Today, news is consumed in radically different ways. In 2022, only 16 per cent of Canadians identified print media as an important source of news. Almost 80 per cent said that they got their news online, mainly through their smartphone. A small proportion of people go directly to websites of news organizations to look for news, and an even smaller proportion pay for access to news sites. Most people link to news stories that they see mentioned in social media, on aggregator websites, or in search engine results. Internationally, it has been estimated that 40 per cent of young adults, those age eighteen to twenty-four, rely on social media platforms as their primary news source. A 2023 survey conducted for the Canadian government suggested that 44 per cent of all Canadians relied on social media platforms for their daily news.

News is not just consumed differently; it is produced and distributed differently too. Canadians are more actively engaged in deciding what counts as a major story, by signalling what they like and dislike. Citizens also help to circulate news and shape the agenda by posting or reposting stories on social media. Sometimes they are actively engaged in content production, by adding comments or uploading video. At the same time, the Internet has created new opportunities for Canadians to act on the news. The possibilities for personal expression and activism are no longer bounded by geography.

Many people watching these transformations over the last quarter-century have talked about "democratization of the news." At first glance it seems as though old elites have been toppled and political power has been distributed more widely among ordinary people. Think of movements in Canada like Idle No More or the Freedom Convoy that have gained more influence over the public agenda because of social media. On closer inspection, however, technological change may simply have replaced the old elite with a new one. Massive corporations – including Google, Meta, and X (formerly Twitter) – now exercise immense influence over the flow of communications between Canadians on questions of public affairs. The platforms owned by these corporations "set the rules for public deliberation." Technological change has had other anti-democratic effects as well. The boundaries of the Canadian public sphere have eroded, and the capacity of Canadians to deliberate constructively has been compromised.

What does it mean to say that the boundaries of the Canadian public sphere have eroded? That foreign actors play a larger role within it, setting the agenda and terms of debate, than they did forty years ago. Corporations like Google and Meta that dominate the search engine and social media business in Canada are foreign-owned. CBC still ran the most popular news website in Canada in 2021, but trust in the public broadcaster has declined markedly. Of the next nine most popular news sites, however, five were American-owned. MSN News had more Canadian traffic in 2021 than either CTV or Global News. In a 2022 survey, Canadians identified the BBC as a more reliable source of news than the *Globe and Mail*, and the *New York Times* as more reliable than the *National Post* or *Toronto Star*.

Harder to measure, but equally important, is the restructuring of social networks that include Canadian citizens. Freed from the constraints of geography, Canadians are more likely to link with like-minded people in other countries. Canadian activists on both the left and right are connected more tightly with peers in the United States. One result is that political developments in the United States – such as the rise of Trump-style populism; Black Lives Matter; the anti-vax and anti-mask movement; and controversies over gun control, abortion rights, and critical race theory – have a faster and stronger echo effect in Canada. Debate within the Canadian public sphere increasingly reflects American rather than Canadian ground realities.

This is not the only sense in which networks have been restructured. Digital transformations have made it easier for immigrant communities to remain connected with their countries of origin. Canada's politics, like its population, has become more cosmopolitan. Controversies in countries like Iran, Syria, India, Ukraine, Israel, and Palestine quickly become controversies in Canada as well. Foreign governments like those of China and Russia have also breached the walls of the Canadian public sphere by launching clandestine disinformation campaigns that are calculated to skew debate to their advantage or simply to corrode goodwill by playing on internal divisions.

DESTABILIZATION OF THE AGENDA

The digital transformation has compromised the Canadian sphere in other ways. Obviously, it has undercut the ability of old elites to set the policy agenda. We might have little sympathy with this change. More problematic is the fact that technological change has undermined the ability of *any* set of actors to set a policy agenda that persists for a reasonable amount of time. It is more difficult for citizens to formulate opinions when the shortlist of important issues that they are supposed to think about changes constantly. Citizens stop trying to formulate opinions when they lack clear signals about what issues matter most.

There is good evidence that this problem of agenda instability afflicts Canada and other democracies. A 2019 study found that the pace at which topics seize collective attention on the Internet and then drop into irrelevance is accelerating and contributing to "more rapid exhaustion of limited attention resources." Acceleration happens because we live in a more complex world but also because key actors, such as the owners of social media platforms, make money by emphasizing novelty rather than continuity.

One result of a destabilized agenda is that citizens feel overwhelmed. "Some days it feels like one major crisis after another," University of Toronto professor Ronald Deibert observed in 2020. "Yesterday's scandal quickly fades into distant memory as viral stories rain down on us continuously." A 2022 cross-national study found that the proportion of citizens who actively avoid the news because it is overwhelming or hard to follow has increased sharply in recent years. A 2023 US survey found that the proportion of adults who follow the news all or most of the time had dropped from 51 per cent to 38 per cent over the preceding six years.

THE THREAT TO CIVIL DISCOURSE

The mere existence of a public sphere, a venue in which Canadians can talk with one another, is not enough to ensure healthy conversation about national priorities. People have to use the public sphere in a certain way. They must pay attention to the conversation for a sustained period of time, work hard at sorting good arguments from bad ones, care about getting facts right, and be open-minded about alternative points of view.

To be fair, there has never been a moment in history when people met these high standards of deliberation. Thinking is hard work, a wit said in 1915, like cutting maple butts with a dull saw. Most Canadians who lived in the twentieth century grew up in small towns plagued by rumour, religious and racial prejudice, and hostility toward expertise. Authors like Stephen Leacock made light of small-town thinking in early twentieth-century Canada, but the realities were darker.

Developments in the late twentieth century – mass communication, the spread of university education, urbanization, and travel – promised an escape from parochialism and prejudice, and the arrival of the Internet in the 1990s seemed like another step along that path. Experts predicted that the Internet would launch a new epoch of democracy in which citizens participated actively in law-making by local and even national governments. James Perry Barlow, an early advocate for the Internet, anticipated that it would produce a new "civilization of the mind" guided by shared concern for the common good.

Rosy expectations about a revolution in democracy have not been realized. One reason is that societal change has left citizens stressed and overwhelmed. A United Nations report suggests this is a global phenomenon: "feelings of distress are on the rise nearly everywhere." In a 2021 Statistics Canada survey, one-fifth of Canadians reported that they found most days quite a bit or extremely stressful. Worries about economic security and blurring of the boundaries between work and home life contribute to stress. Even before the pandemic, 40 per cent of Canadian workers said that they had more work and family obligations than they could handle satisfactorily. Justice Paul Rouleau, who led the 2022 Freedom Convoy inquiry, concluded that economic anxieties compounded by the pandemic were an important trigger for that protest.

New information technologies have aggravated stress too. Almost all Canadians now use some form of social media, on average almost two hours a day. Such heavy usage is no accident. Social media platforms make money by keeping users on their sites as long as possible; they use "attention engineering" to encourage addictive behaviour by exploiting frailties of human psychology. A 2023 lawsuit by forty American state governments against Meta alleged that the company knowingly designed its platforms to promote "compulsive, prolonged, and unhealthy use" by "capitaliz[ing] on young users' dopamine responses." Research shows that frequent users of social media feel separation anxiety when they are denied access to their electronic devices for only a few minutes. A 2018 Statistics Canada survey found that heavy use of social media contributed to loss of sleep, trouble concentrating on tasks, and feelings of anxiety or depression. These effects were more pronounced among young Canadians.

Effective deliberation takes time and thoughtfulness. On any significant question of public policy, arguments for one position or another are rarely decisive. One virtue of a world dominated by print media is that it demanded concentration and thoughtfulness by citizens. Reading is usually solitary work: readers sit by themselves to decode long passages of text. By contrast, social media actively discourages citizens from focusing on any one issue for too long. Platforms encourage impulsive responses to complex problems. We live in a world in which pundits are expected to have a "hot take" on every issue. We like or dislike and quickly move on.

Deliberation also requires a willingness to engage with people who have different ideas. At one point it seemed as though the Internet would actually improve our ability to do this. Mark Zuckerberg, founder of Facebook, promised that the platform would "strengthen our social fabric and bring the world closer together." As late as 2009, technology expert Clay Shirky thought it reasonable to say, "The internet runs on love."

We know better today. Canada's former governor general David Johnston lamented in 2022 that "the digital age of instant communication … amplifies anger [and] stokes fear." In a 2021 survey, a large majority of Canadian residents reported seeing hate speech or some other form of harmful content on the Internet in the past month. A study of tweets received by incumbent candidates in the 2021 Canadian federal election found that one-fifth were toxic, mainly because they contained insults, threats, or profanity. Female politicians are disproportionately targeted by hate-fuelled comments on social media. "I have received non-stop abuse on Twitter," Green Party leader Elizabeth May said in 2023, including death threats every day.

Johnston's successor as governor general, Mary Simon, announced in 2023 that she would close her social media posts to comments because of the rise in "abusive, misogynistic, and racist engagement ... including a greater number of violent threats."

Deliberation also requires a respect for the truth, and this too is under threat. In some countries, politicians and their supporters have learned that they can win power through massive, technology-driven disinformation campaigns. The deluge of falsehoods increases the burden on citizens to separate fact from fiction. In a 2023 Statistics Canada survey, 43 per cent of Canadians said it was harder to distinguish between true and false information than it was three years earlier.

In fact, Internet-driven engagement may actively discourage citizens from doing this sort of work. As cultural theorist Byung-Chul Han suggests, individuals may subscribe to conspiracy theories or other falsehoods as a way of affirming their membership in a "digital tribe" that provides a sense of community in a stress-filled world. Precisely because belief becomes a marker of identity and solidarity, it may become unshakeable.

A 2022 Abacus survey found that conspiracy theories are becoming more deeply rooted in Canadian politics. Nearly one in three adult Canadians were prepared to believe that it was possibly or probably true that Microsoft founder Bill Gates is using microchip implants to track people and control their behaviour. Social media, Justice Rouleau concluded in 2023, worked like "an accelerant for misinformation and disinformation" in months leading up to the Freedom Convoy protest. He urged Canadian governments to examine the "serious challenges" that social media posed to Canadian society.

POLICY KNOWLEDGE AND THE DECLINE OF NEWS

Effective deliberation in the Canadian public sphere requires more than attention and good faith. It also requires policy knowledge – that is, knowledge about challenges facing the country and how they could be handled. But this, too, may be in short supply.

In theory, parties could serve as an important source of policy knowledge for citizens. But as I said in chapter 3, parties have limited capacity to formulate their own views about long-term challenges and are increasingly focused on short-term politics. "The core of the party organization is concerned primarily with elections," the Lortie Royal Commission on Electoral Reform and Party Financing observed in 1991. "It is much less interested in discussing and analysing political issues that are not connected directly to winning the next election, or in attempting to articulate the broader values of the party." This statement remains true today.

For many citizens, another critical source of policy knowledge has been professional journalism. Professional journalists play three critical roles. One role, important but overemphasized, is exposing government misconduct. Another is translating the work of officials and experts so that it makes sense to citizens. A third is putting events in context and explaining what matters – that is, telling the bigger story that connects today's news to the past and to the future. We expect professional journalists to respect principles such as impartiality, thoroughness, accuracy, and fairness.

These are twentieth-century ideals. The concept of professional journalism was largely unknown in the nineteenth century, the era of yellow journalism. The United States only got its first school for training journalists in 1908, and Canada in 1945. Raising standards for news reporting was an essential part of the progressive program for "bettering democracy" in the early twentieth century. "The present crisis of Western democracy," American writer Walter Lippmann said in 1920, "is a crisis in journalism." Professional journalism became possible mainly because newspapers were making enough money through subscriptions and advertising to provide journalists with a living wage and give them some freedom in doing their work. Later, broadcasters were able to do the same.

In the twenty-first century, however, technological change has caused a collapse in newspaper and broadcasting revenues. Earnings of Canadian newspapers plummeted from $5.4 billion in 2006 to $2.7 billion in 2018. By 2020, the first year of the COVID pandemic, revenues had dropped again to $2.1 billion. Less revenue means less money to pay workers. The wage bill of Canadian newspapers declined by 60 per cent between 2006 and 2020.

Advertising revenue has been scooped up by digital enterprises like Google and Facebook, now rebranded as Meta. Digital advertising revenues in Canada increased to $12 billion in 2021, 70 per cent of which was harvested by search engines and social media platforms. But Google and Meta do not see themselves as producers of news, and they are not in the business of providing journalists with a living wage.

The result is a crisis of professional journalism, in Canada as in the United States. There were about ten thousand working journalists in Canada in 2021, down from a historic peak of thirteen thousand in 2011. The country now has the same number of journalists as it had forty years ago, even though the growth in population, government spending, and economic activity, among other factors, has increased the amount of news to be covered. Moreover, a larger proportion of today's journalists work as freelancers rather than full-time employees at news organizations.

One result of the crisis in journalism is a dramatic reduction in coverage of public affairs. In Ottawa, the parliamentary press gallery is the smallest that it has been in thirty years. The *Toronto Star* had ten staff listed as members of the parliamentary press gallery in Ottawa in 1994, while the *Ottawa Citizen* had twelve; today, the *Star* has seven, while the *Citizen* has two. Many regional newspapers have closed their Ottawa bureaus entirely, relying more on news services like the Canadian Press. The Canadian Press itself cut staff in Ottawa by two-thirds between the late 1980s and 2020.

The same story is repeated in provincial capitals. In Ontario, for example, forty journalists were assigned to the provincial press gallery in 1975. By 2017, there were only twenty-five, even though provincial government spending had more than tripled in real terms in that period. And the situation is even more dire in smaller communities. Across the country, almost three hundred community newspapers were closed between 2011 and 2020. A 2018 study by the Public Policy

Forum described the consequences: a dramatic decline in news about democratic institutions and civic affairs in those communities.

Not only has the amount of news about public affairs declined. So has the quality. The 2018 Public Policy Forum study found that local news, where it is available, gives less attention to opposing views, historical context, and supporting data. Lacking time to develop their own stories or probe what they are given, journalists are more likely to react to events, follow the pack, or simply retransmit news as it is packaged by businesses or government agencies. During the 2019 federal election, professor April Lindgren noted a "proliferation of superficial journalism," with overwhelmed reporters "often reduced to repurposing press releases and grabbing quotes from politicians' social-media posts."

In fact, the balance of forces between journalists and spin doctors in the public and private sectors has shifted dramatically over the last forty years. In 1987, Canada had one full-time journalist for every four people employed in advertising, marketing, and public relations. Today, the ratio is one to twelve.

INADEQUACY OF OUR CIVIC AND HISTORICAL KNOWLEDGE

Policy knowledge is not the only prerequisite for informed debate. Citizens also need historical knowledge of a particular kind: about the path that the country has followed and the challenges it has confronted in the past. And they need civic knowledge, about Canadian governmental institutions and how they work. In these two areas, Canadians know less than they should.

Frustration among historians about the limitations of Canadians' historical knowledge is decades old. Thirty years ago, Michael Bliss claimed that lack of historical understanding was contributing to a "withering of a sense of community" in Canada. Soon after, J.L. Granatstein said that Canada was becoming "a nation without memory … every bit adrift as an amnesiac wandering the streets." Canadians, Desmond Morton agreed in 2002, "do not know most of the elementary facts about their history. Ignorance is commonplace."

A battery of polls provides evidence that Canadians know too little about their history and system of government. In a 2006 survey, most Canadians could not name a single cabinet minister, other than the prime minister, and scarcely half could identify the opposition party. In a 2023 survey that ranked prime ministers, Canadians largely overlooked anyone outside living memory. In a 2007 Dominion Institute survey of young adults, most respondents could not name Canada's first prime minister or the year of Confederation. In another survey, most respondents said incorrectly that the Canadian prime minister is directly elected. In yet another, respondents were better at identifying the longest-serving American president (Franklin Roosevelt) than they were the longest-serving Canadian prime minister (William Lyon Mackenzie King) – although a large majority could not identify either one.

Not everyone is appalled by these survey results. Some complain that survey questions like these are pedantic. Does it really matter, after all, that only one in twenty Quebecers can name the first premier of their province? This complaint has some merit. We should really be concerned about understanding of the broad lines of Canadian history, rather than names and dates – but survey questions are not good for testing general knowledge, so name-and-date questions must serve as a proxy. And Canadians themselves concede that their general knowledge is not good. In 2022 surveys conducted for the Association for Canadian Studies, for example, almost 60 per cent of respondents said that they were not knowledgeable about World War I, almost 50 per cent that they were not knowledgeable about World War II, and more than 40 per cent that they had little or no knowledge about Indigenous peoples.

Critics also protest that these surveys are intended to serve an essentially conservative political agenda. For example, why so many questions about political leaders like John A. Macdonald, disgraced in some eyes because of his treatment of Indigenous peoples? In 1998, J.L. Granatstein argued that historical understanding was necessary for Canada to become one nation, founded on European cultural traditions. But what if we reject the premise that Canada ought to be a single nation or that European traditions are central to its history?

We should be clear why historical knowledge matters in the present context. We are not concerned here with the cultivation of patriotism or a common sense of nationality. Our interest is adaptability, and our concern is whether citizens have the knowledge necessary to decide how the country can survive and thrive in coming decades. To reach a decision about what survival requires, a sense of the country's history is necessary. We look at the past to understand how future challenges might be managed. With that purpose in mind, we do not need to honour the past or agree on one grand narrative of national progress.

History is a survival guide, a playbook for preserving a community. This is an old idea. Professor Michael Marker has observed that Indigenous communities preserved their histories because "people made important survival decisions" based on stories about what happened in the past. "A wrongly told story," Marker said, "could have devastating consequences." Niccolò Machiavelli, writing in the early sixteenth century, took the same view: "[We examine] past events carefully to foresee future events … and to apply the remedies that the ancients employed, or if old remedies cannot be found, to think of new ones based upon the similarity of circumstances." Professor Ken Osborne has argued that "we are in the stream of history whether we like it or not, and if we are to negotiate its currents successfully, we need the kind of navigation guide that a knowledge of history can provide."

Remember, too, that surveys reveal a lack of civic knowledge as well as historical knowledge. A recent civics textbook laments "Canadians' general ignorance" of the principles that undergird the Canadian system of government. Sometimes, Canadians assume that their government is built on the same principles as American government. This is like using a Microsoft manual to operate an Apple computer.

Signs of confusion about the workings of Canadian government are easily found. In 2022, Freedom Convoy protesters appealed to the Speaker of the Senate to lift vaccine mandates, describing him as one of "the highest authorities representing the Federal Government." This might be true of the US Senate's majority leader, but not of Canada's Senate Speaker. Other protesters condemned Justin Trudeau's behaviour as Canada's head of state: but Canadian prime ministers, unlike American presidents, are not heads of state. Later in 2022, Alberta premier Danielle Smith promised to "issue pardons" to pandemic protesters: but Canadian premiers, unlike American governors, lack this authority. "I am more convinced than ever," journalist Mercedes Stephenson said while reporting on the Rouleau inquiry in 2022, "that we need to do a better job across this country of dedicating time and resources to civics classes on how government works."

Lack of historical and civic knowledge cannot be blamed mainly on technological change. A more direct explanation is the failure of government policy. Courses on history and civics get short shrift in school systems across the country. Canada is unique among Western countries because it has no federal office of education and no national educational policy. Provinces alone decide what is taught in their public schools. A 2021 cross-country study found that almost all provinces were "struggling to provide a more comprehensive review of the country's history." Only four of thirteen provinces and territories require that high school students complete a history course. In Ontario, the province that receives the highest ranking for attention to history, there is still a "yawning absence of history in early grades."

Time for courses on history and civics has been squeezed as schools put more emphasis on science, technology, and employable skills. Even when history courses are offered, they may focus on modes of historical reasoning, rather than the substance of Canadian history, a subject that is more likely to draw controversy. Researchers at University of New Brunswick observed in 2010 that Canada remains a "dabbler" in citizenship education, unique among major democracies because of its "complete lack of national debate or policy initiative" on the subject. Professor Alan Sears said in 2023 that Canada has "missed opportunities to participate in international studies of civic education … [and] neglected to build any substantial research capacity in citizenship education."

There is also a limit to what history and civic education in elementary and high schools can do. The average Canadian, forty-three years old, is unlikely to remember much of what they were taught thirty years earlier, and a large part of what they were taught may now be outmoded. Meanwhile, hundreds of thousands of new Canadians arrive as adult immigrants each year. Although federal and provincial governments provide transition assistance to new immigrants, this is focused on immediate problems like finding work and housing. The federal government does provide help to applicants in preparing for the citizenship knowledge test, but the federal role in civic education for adults has traditionally ended when people become citizens. (In fact, a 2007 survey suggested that most native-born Canadians would fail to pass the rudimentary requirements of the citizenship knowledge test.)

In the past, political parties also played a role in educating citizens about how government works. As the Lortie Commission observed in its 1991 report, the constituency associations of political parties were once important parts of community life, with a large number of dedicated members. But constituency associations have withered away like other community organizations. The commission observed that power was shifting within Canadian parties from constituency associations to headquarters, while party membership was shrinking and becoming less consequential. Party members were corralled to vote at critical moments but did little else. These trends accelerated after 1991. Today, individuals become members of the Liberal Party of Canada simply by entering their email address on the party website or making a single donation to the party.

A CONFUSED FEDERAL RESPONSE

After 2015, the government of Justin Trudeau adopted several policies that may have helped to repair the quality of political conversation in Canada, although these policies were not always justified in those terms. Soon after its election, the Trudeau government reversed Harper-era cuts to the CBC. In 2018 it launched the Local Journalism Initiative, a five-year program to promote "civic journalism for underserved communities." The following year, it gave tax breaks to organizations employing journalists and to Canadians who subscribe to digital news, and allowed news organizations that converted to non-profit status to claim more favourable tax treatment. These measures were expected to cost about $130 million a year.

During the pandemic, described as a "six-alarm fire" for media outlets, the federal government provided emergency assistance through wage subsidies and increased advertising. And in 2023, it adopted Bill C-18, the Online News Act, which requires digital platforms like Google and Meta to pay Canadian media outlets when they publish links to news stories. The law was expected to generate about $300 million in revenue for news businesses in Canada. In addition, the federal government has undertaken small projects to promote digital media literacy, taken steps to counter foreign disinformation campaigns, and promised legislation to curb hate speech on the Internet.

Many of these initiatives have been criticized. Experts have complained that federal programs are simply bailouts for obsolete industries or contrarily that they are too small to do much for media outlets that have seen a multibillion-dollar decline in revenues. Some reforms have suffered from serious design flaws and weak implementation. The biggest initiative, the Online News Act adopted in June 2023, seemed to backfire when Meta announced that it would block Canadian news stories entirely, and Google threatened to do the same. The federal government settled with Google in November 2023, but the financial contribution that Google promised to Canadian news outlets was less than expected. No agreement with Meta had been reached by the end of 2023.

The Conservative opposition assaulted many of these policies. Conservative leader Pierre Poilievre promised to "defund the CBC," calling it "Trudeau propaganda," and opposed tax relief for other journalism organizations, suggesting that new tax rules gave Liberal ministers the power to "shut down" media asking "uncomfortable questions." In 2023, Poilievre waved a copy of George Orwell's *1984* in the House of Commons as he criticized a media reform bill and condemned the federal agency responsible for implementing the Online News Act as "a woke agency … named by Liberals." All this was part of Poilievre's populist campaign to put Canadians "back in control" of their country.

Poilievre's rhetoric upended the traditional way of thinking about media policy in Canada. In the twentieth century, federal action to support the public sphere had been justified as a way of putting Canadians "back in control." In the eyes of reformers from that time, governmental inaction would not make Canadians freer, either individually or collectively. It would simply undermine Canadian sovereignty, by allowing foreign media to dictate the terms of political debate in Canada.

Most Conservative supporters backed Poilievre's attacks on Trudeau policies. But a minority still followed the old logic of media reform. A former communications director for Stephen Harper, Andrew McDougall, dismissed Poilievre's attacks on the CBC as "juvenile." National politics, McDougall said, requires "some sort of common understanding … to function properly," but the digital revolution has left the Canadian public "scattered all over the place … watching and experiencing different things." McDougall concluded that there was a Conservative argument for reforming the CBC rather than defunding it, to preserve "our national fabric."

There were moments when Liberal spokespeople also invoked the old logic of media reform to justify their policies. "We are standing up for our independence," said Heritage Minister Pablo Rodriguez in June 2023, as the Online News Act became law. "We are standing up for our sovereignty, and we are standing up for our democracy." Justin Trudeau took the same line in July 2023, after Meta announced it would block Canadian news. "This is a dispute over democracy," Trudeau said. "This goes to the core of a free and informed society that is able to take responsible decisions." But such full-throated defences of federal initiatives were the exception rather than the rule. Liberal statements about their policy objectives were usually framed differently, and often diffidently.

This alternate framing was evident in Liberal Party platforms, the lodestone of government policy. While the 2015 Liberal platform made promises about improving democracy, these were focused mainly on reforming elections and institutions in Ottawa. The platform said nothing about news or Internet regulation and described the proposed increase in CBC funding as an investment in "cultural and creative industries." In the 2019 platform, CBC funding and Canadian-content requirements for streaming services were again presented as "arts and culture" measures, while proposed anti-hate speech legislation featured as an initiative to promote equality and diversity. In its 2021 platform, the party counted the proposed Online News Act as another arts-and-culture policy and described its Local Journalism Initiative as a tool for "empowering racialized journalists" rather than improving coverage of civic affairs.

The same framing of Liberal policies was evident in mandate letters given to new ministers. Most responsibility for media-related policies under the Trudeau government was held by the minister of Canadian Heritage. "Your overarching goal," Trudeau told his first Heritage minister, Mélanie Joly, "will be to implement our government's plan to strengthen our cultural and creative industries." Her successor, Pablo Rodriguez, was told that his priorities should be to promote cultural and creative industries and "celebrate Canada's diversity and foster greater inclusion." His successor, Steven Guilbeault, was directed to "celebrate Canada's heritage," promote cultural and creative industries, and support amateur sports. When Rodriguez resumed the portfolio in 2021, he was instructed that his immediate priority should be to "ensure that artists and cultural industries have the supports they need" during the COVID pandemic.

As I said in chapter 2, prime ministers have wide discretion to restructure federal departments to reflect their goals. But there was no significant change in the purpose and structure of Canadian Heritage when Liberals took power in 2015. "Our mission," Heritage Minister Joly said in her first annual report, "is to promote an environment in which all Canadians take full advantage of dynamic cultural experiences, celebrate our history and heritage, and participate in building creative communities." Democracy and sovereignty were not mentioned. Eight years later, Canadian Heritage still defined its five "core responsibilities" as "creativity, arts and culture; heritage and celebration; sport; diversity and inclusion; [and] official languages."

From the point of view of political tactics, placing media reform efforts in a box labelled "arts and culture" was a mistake. It increased the probability of a populist assault on these policies. By 2015, Conservative skepticism about federal arts and culture policies was well established. In 2008, Stephen Harper had dismissed federal cultural programs as handouts for a spoiled elite, rather than something that mattered to "ordinary working people." Too often, Harper said, the federal government was "funding things that people don't want." Poilievre carried on the tradition of skepticism about cultural programs and applied it to the Liberals' media reforms, now also labelled as arts-and-culture initiatives.

But we should not dwell just on tactics. The larger point is that the Canada public sphere slid into crisis after the early 2000s. The capacity of Canadians to engage constructively with one another was rapidly undermined, mainly but not exclusively because of technological change. Canadians were indeed losing control of their country, in the sense that it was harder to have a productive conversation about national priorities. But this crisis was not properly named or addressed directly. Policy-makers managed bits and pieces of the crisis, sometimes impulsively. Because there had never been adequate public discussion of the overall problem, there was little agreement about how to handle it. As a result, policy responses were enveloped in confusion and controversy.

How did Canada fall into this predicament? Maybe this is what happens when a country backs away from investment in forward-thinking. For example, a royal commission might have been appointed to look at the impact of technological and social change, as had been done many times in the past. This might have produced deeper public understanding and broader agreement about the nature of the problem and potential solutions. But royal commissions were dismissed as slow and unreliable. Independent councils might also have looked at the problem, but they had been cut back too. Policy capacity in departments has also been reduced, and in any case, departments have been sidelined by political parties, which also lack capacity for robust policy development.

In addition to all this, Canada might have been caught in a vicious circle in the twenty-first century. As the public sphere decays, the ability to think constructively about the condition of the public sphere may also decay. The same stresses and strains that make it harder to reach agreement on any problem, make it hard to reach agreement on reforms that might preserve the possibility of a constructive national conversation. A collapse in the quality of the national conversation would be fatal for adaptability as well as democracy. But it might be avoided, as I suggest in chapter 7.

The Web of Rules

6

In 2022, the federal public service comprised 357,000 people, working in ninety departments and agencies. Many of these organizations are small, though. Almost 90 per cent of public servants work in the twenty-five largest organizations. The service is led by an executive group of about 9,000 people.

In the abstract, federal public servants, like their counterparts in other levels of Canadian government, could help to improve adaptability of the overall political system in two ways. They could contribute to policy development by anticipating risks, defining problems, and inventing potential responses to those problems. And public servants play a critical role in policy implementation – that is, translating ideas into action.

In the middle of the twentieth century, senior public servants in Ottawa often played a central, perhaps dominant, role in policy development. But the days of these powerful bureaucratic mandarins are long gone. We should be glad about this because that mandarin class did not reflect the diversity of Canada's population. They were mainly white male anglophones, disproportionately from central Canada.

As we saw in chapter 3, the style of platform governance that has emerged over the last thirty years has shrunk the policy role of the federal public service even further. In this new style of governance, parties make policy commitments while public servants focus on delivery. This shift in roles is worrisome because parties in Canada today lack the capacity to make policy well. Public servants believe that their expertise is neglected and that the quality of national policy suffers as a result.

In addition, there are concerns about the capacity of federal departments and agencies to implement policy competently. These worries are not entirely new. Even in the 1970s, some observers thought that the federal public service was losing its agility. A committee established to review the public service in 1979 lamented "slavish adherence to detailed and increasing regulation" within federal departments and an environment in which managers lacked authority "to make decisions (and mistakes)." Historian J.L. Granatstein observed in 1982, "The huge bureaucracy that is the civil service of today is formal and rigid. Decisions are slow and grudging, initiative is blocked, procedures are everything."

This perception of the public service as a creaky machine has deepened over time. A distinguished observer of Canadian government, Donald Savoie, concluded in 2019 that the public service had degraded into a "cautious, uncertain institution." Paul Tellier, once the most senior public servant in Ottawa, warned in 2022 that a "culture of risk-aversion" was deeply entrenched within the federal public service. One of his successors, Kevin Lynch, writing with former executive Jim Mitchell, agreed in 2023 that there is now "an operating culture of control and risk avoidance." Risk-aversion, another senior executive said in a 2022 study, has become "a core feature of the system."

Risk-aversion reveals itself in several ways. Public servants avoid unorthodox decisions, even when they have authority to deviate from standard practice and it makes sense in the circumstances. They avoid actions with unpredictable and potentially controversial outcomes and organize their decision-making so that responsibility for bad outcomes is diffused. Public servants are less forthright in advice to ministers and more accommodating when political staff make inappropriate demands on the public service. And public servants may not sound the alarm when policies are clearly headed for failure.

Complaints about risk-aversion within the public service should not be accepted uncritically. The federal bureaucracy still moves quickly and creatively in moments of crisis, as it did during the COVID pandemic. Nimbleness is possible because many of the usual controls are loosened for the duration of the crisis. Politicians focus on results rather than process. When the emergency passes, however, the public service seems to snap back to its usual state.

There is another reason to be wary of the risk-aversion diagnosis. It confuses a symptom with the underlying disease. Public servants are risk-averse for good reasons. The architecture of the federal public service has changed in two important ways, both of which induce more cautious behaviour.

First, public servants are subject to more administrative controls than they once were. More rules inevitably mean an increased likelihood of rule violations, whether accidental or deliberate. Many of these controls are now overseen by independent watchdogs, which increases the likelihood that rule violations will be exposed. Because the political world has become more volatile, controversies about rule violations escalate quickly, so that public servants find themselves suddenly in the hot seat. Understanding these realities, public servants step carefully.

There is a second structural change that encourages risk-aversion. The number of political staff who supervise the bureaucracy on behalf of ministers has grown substantially over the last forty years. Without much thought or planning, a new institution – what we might call the political service – has come into existence in Ottawa. It has its own culture, which is preoccupied with crisis avoidance and message discipline. Political staff have extensive influence over the public service, which they sometimes wield arbitrarily. Public servants behave cautiously so they do not run afoul of political staff.

Another shift in Ottawa politics has compounded the woes of the federal public service. For much of the twentieth century, federal governments routinely established independent commissions to check the health of the public service and recommend housekeeping reforms. Unfortunately, this form of routine maintenance faded in the twenty-first century. The result is that cracks in the foundation of the public service are less likely to be repaired properly. Preserving the health of the public service is just like performing upkeep on buildings and bridges. It is hard work that yields long-term benefits. Politicians with an eye on the short run are less likely to do it.

ACCRETION OF ADMINISTRATIVE CONTROLS

In 2009, a blue-ribbon advisory committee told Prime Minister Stephen Harper that the public service was enmeshed in a "web of rules" that limited its ability to get work done. This is right to a point. Certainly, there are rules – some laid down in statutes passed by Parliament, some drafted and enforced by central agencies like the Treasury Board Secretariat, and some manufactured by departments and agencies themselves. But there are not just rules. Over the years, the federal government has created a series of independent bodies that are charged with monitoring the public service to assure compliance with the rules. The control regime for the federal public service consists of rules and watchdog organizations. This regime is bolstered by a powerful political dynamic that I describe later.

The oldest of these watchdog organizations is the Office of the Auditor General (OAG), established in 1878. Like other watchdogs, the auditor general is accountable to Parliament and not the prime minister. In the beginning the OAG interpreted its role narrowly. It checked that expenditures by public servants were properly documented and authorized by law. Over time, however, the OAG's focus broadened. In the 1960s, the OAG began looking at bigger questions about efficiency in federal departments, and its reports became media events, as they still are today. The OAG "sets forth the sins, errors and omissions of government departments," the *Canadian Weekly* explained in 1964, "and then all hell breaks loose."

In 1977, Parliament approved a "vast expansion" of the OAG's authority, giving it broad discretion to judge whether federal departments were producing "value for money." Professor Sharon Sutherland said that the 1977 law enabled the OAG to behave like "a government in exile." A recent review of OAG reports produced since 2000 found that they often used a "combative" style of communication, "making greater use of words evoking negative emotions such as anger, disgust, fear, and sadness" in an attempt to attract the attention of journalists and the broader public.

The second oldest watchdog, the Public Service Commission, had sweeping authority over the public service almost from the start. It was originally established in 1908 as the Civil Service Commission, to reduce political influence over hiring and promotion within the public service. Its authority grew immensely in 1918, when the government of Robert Borden, struggling to manage a wartime bureaucracy, hired Chicago consultant Edwin O. Griffenhagen to overhaul its personnel system.

The 1918 reforms were well-intended but excessive. Griffenhagen assumed wrongly that Canada's government was as corrupt as Chicago's. As a result, Parliament adopted a law that nearly eliminated the discretion of departmental leaders over organization, compensation, hiring, promotion, and firing. Senior public servants complained that it was impossible to get work done, and in the following decades, governments made repeated attempts to loosen the 1918 controls. The personnel system is now more decentralized than at its founding, but it is still complex, and the commission continues to play an important oversight role. After the latest reforms in 2003, its independence was strengthened and its auditing staff expanded. The commission's head at the time said that its ambition was to emulate the auditor general, "shaming and blaming" departments when it believed that the merit principle was being disrespected.

Attempts to lighten regulation by the Public Service Commission were offset by the addition of other controls. In 1967, Parliament allowed federal workers to unionize and created a system of collective bargaining. The union movement has weakened in Canada's private sector since the 1960s but has grown stronger in the public sector. The process of collective bargaining, "complex and time-consuming," is overseen by another independent body, the Federal Public Sector Labour Relations and Employment Board. The board also investigates grievances from individual employees that cannot be resolved within the public service. In 2022 it was managing a caseload of almost six thousand files.

For much of its history, the federal public service was dominated by English-speaking Canadians. The Official Languages Act, adopted in 1969, was designed to remedy this injustice. The public service was directed to provide public services in English and French and to assure that francophones had equal opportunity for employment and promotion. In some parts of the country, federal employees also have the right to work in either language. Another independent watchdog, the Commissioner of Official Languages, was created to monitor compliance with this law.

In 1977, Parliament established the Canadian Human Rights Commission, with a mandate to receive complaints about discrimination within the federal public service and other organizations within federal jurisdiction. At the same time, Parliament created a sixth independent body, the Privacy Commissioner of Canada, to oversee the handling of personal information collected from Canadians by the federal public service and to receive complaints about non-compliance with that law.

In 1982, the Charter of Rights and Freedoms was added to the Canadian Constitution. This affected the public service in several ways. Proposed legislation must now be reviewed by the Department of Justice to anticipate potential infringements of citizens' rights. The Charter also strengthens the hand of citizens who believe that they have been denied benefits or services by federal departments without a fair hearing. Public servants themselves use the Charter to challenge workplace rules such as restrictions on political activity. Ultimately, courts determine what the Charter requires, and since 1982 they have scrutinized the work of federal public servants more closely.

The Charter was followed in 1983 by the Access to Information Act, which gives Canadians a right to obtain documents held within federal departments and agencies. An information commissioner, another independent parliamentary officer, was appointed to receive public complaints about non-compliance with the law. A comparable American law, the Freedom of Information Act, was once described as "the Taj Mahal of unintended consequences," and the same could be said about the Canadian law. It frustrates officials and citizens alike. A 2000 study found that the average information request consumed one workweek of labour, and that the total cost of compliance was about $40 million a year. Another study twenty years later estimated that compliance costs had increased fivefold, to nearly $200 million a year.

In 1989 Parliament adopted legislation to regulate lobbying of the federal government. The law was strengthened in 1998. It complicates the relationship between public servants and outsiders because communication between the two could trigger a duty to report to the new registrar of lobbyists. The Chrétien government also adopted ethics rules for senior public servants, overseen by an ethics counsellor, that included additional reporting requirements as well as restrictions on the kind of work that could be done after leaving public service.

In 1995, Parliament extended the powers of the Canadian Human Rights Commission so that it could monitor the progress of federal departments and agencies in improving diversity within the federal workforce. In the same year, Parliament created yet another independent watchdog, the commissioner of the environment and sustainable development, to monitor the progress of federal departments toward sustainable development goals. Environment Minister Sheila Copps hoped that the new office would generate the same "blaze of publicity that attends each auditor general's report of financial failings." Citizens can petition the commissioner when departments neglect environmental concerns, and departments are required to respond within 120 days.

In January 2000, Canada's Minister of Human Resources Development Jane Stewart released an internal audit that disclosed problems of incomplete documentation in federal programs that provided aid to the unemployed. Opposition politicians quickly called this the "biggest scandal in Canadian history," claiming that as much as $1 billion had been lost. The auditor general blasted the department,

HRDC, for creating "an environment that emphasized service rather than basic controls." The scandal dominated Ottawa for months.

Later investigation showed that actual losses to the government were dramatically lower, about $85,000. By this time, however, the department had cancelled the program and introduced "one of the most extensive and elaborate project review and monitoring systems ever implemented in the federal government." Every new grant required the completion of twenty-four additional forms. Other departments adopted similar controls. In HRDC alone, these new controls cost about $50 million annually.

Another scandal erupted in 2002, when the auditor general found evidence of misconduct in a program intended to raise the visibility of the federal government in Quebec following the 1995 secession referendum. Again, critics called this the biggest scandal in Canadian history. News reports suggested that $100 million of federal money might have been misspent. Prime Minister Paul Martin appointed a commission of inquiry, which concluded in 2005 that financial losses were a small fraction of the original estimate. The inquiry itself cost $70 million.

The head of the inquiry, Justice John Gomery, warned Canadians against concluding that federal government was rife with corruption and carelessness. "The vast majority of our public officials and politicians," he said, "do their work honestly, diligently and effectively." And as Gomery pointed out, the system had rooted out and punished misconduct: "The persons responsible for these irregularities have been identified and reproached for their errors and misconduct. The procedure for uncovering wrongdoing is ponderous and expensive, but in the long run it works fairly well."

The Martin government certainly paid a price for the scandal. It was ousted in a general election eleven weeks after the release of Gomery's report. Liberals would not regain power for another nine years. But the "Gomery effect," as it came to be known, lingered on. The Conservative Party led by Stephen Harper did not share Gomery's view that the system worked well in general. During the 2006 election, Harper insisted that Ottawa was plagued by a culture of "waste, mismanagement, and corruption." He promised sweeping reforms to clean up the federal government.

The Federal Accountability Act of 2006 was the biggest single expansion of the administrative control apparatus since reform of the civil service in 1918. Restrictions on lobbying were stiffened, and enforcement was put in the hands of a new officer of Parliament, the commissioner of lobbying. Another parliamentary officer, the ethics and conflict of interest commissioner, was appointed to oversee tougher ethics rules. A third officer, the public sector integrity commissioner, was authorized to investigate complaints from government employees about wrongdoing within departments. A procurement ombudsman was established to monitor the contracting practices of departments and receive complaints about contracting abuses. A new parliamentary budget officer was charged with undertaking independent assessments of the government's budget plans.

The Accountability Act also made an important change in the division of responsibilities between ministers and deputy ministers. According to parliamentary tradition, the minister alone was responsible to the House of Commons for everything done by their department. The 2006 law made deputy ministers directly accountable to parliamentary committees for questions about compliance with government policies and procedures. Deputy ministers were required to establish independent audit committees to monitor "compliance risks" within their departments. A 2022 study describes a subsequent "audit explosion" within the federal government. The volume of auditing and evaluation work increased fourfold between 2000 and 2019, with audits reflecting "a growing preoccupation with compliance, performance, and risk."

The Harper government fell in 2015, replaced by the Liberal government of Justin Trudeau. Trudeau promised his government would not "interfere with the work of government watchdogs," and in fact it went further than simple non-interference. The parliamentary budget officer was given stronger guarantees of independence and new authority to study party platforms. The information commissioner was given more power to resolve complaints about non-compliance with the Access to Information Act, while departments lost their ability to charge fees for processing information requests. The authority of the environment commissioner was expanded to include oversight of climate change policies.

Meanwhile, the Canadian Human Rights Commission was bolstered with two new officers. An accessibility commissioner became responsible for monitoring compliance with the Accessible Canada Act, a 2019 law which requires federal departments and other organizations to establish plans for removing barriers to work and services for disabled persons. Similarly, a new pay equity commissioner became responsible for monitoring compliance with the Pay Equity Act, which requires the federal government develop a plan for correcting gender-based salary discrimination throughout the public service.

The Liberal government did not act on its promise to establish an advertising commissioner to prevent abuses in government advertising programs, but it did adopt new internal controls, along with a commitment to independent review of larger programs by a non-governmental group, Advertising Standards Canada. The Trudeau government added another system of internal reporting across the public service as part of its effort to track progress in fulfilling the promises contained in its 2015 platform.

WHY MORE CONTROLS?

The burden of administrative controls on the federal public service is undoubtedly heavier than it was forty or fifty years ago. There are more rules constraining the behaviour of public servants, more procedures within the public service for monitoring compliance with these rules, and more independent watchdogs who are responsible for making sure that rules are taken seriously.

There are four reasons for the increasing complexity of this control system. One is the growth in size of the federal public service. By the end of the 1970s, the public service was eight times larger than it was immediately before World War II, comprising almost three hundred thousand people. In a system this large, more rules were inevitable.

It was impossible to keep the machine running properly by relying only on common sense and everyday oversight by senior managers. However, growth by itself cannot explain the complexity of today's control system. By number of employees, the public service of 2024 is not significantly larger than the public service of 1978.

Our rising standards have also contributed to complexity. The public service of the 1960s might have been nimbler but it was fraught with injustices too. As I have noted, senior levels of the public service were dominated at that time by English-speaking white males. Most Canadians did not see themselves represented within this powerful institution. At the same time, there were fewer checks against arbitrary decision-making within the public service. Many of the rules that we have established since the 1970s have been intended to remedy these injustices.

And while our standards have risen, our trust in government has declined. This is another reason for the accretion of rules. When a report of misconduct becomes public, we are more likely to suspect that it is only the tip of the iceberg and less likely to believe that the system will correct mistakes on its own.

The fourth reason for increasing complexity is electoral competition. Party leaders seek votes by appealing to our rising expectations and declining trust. They promise to impose controls that will eliminate injustices and prevent waste and corruption. As political competition intensifies and a party's hold on power becomes more tenuous, the incentive to promise more controls increases.

Political parties have seized on a specific device, the independent watchdog, as a key component of many new control schemes. We could imagine control without watchdogs. For example, we could strengthen parliamentary committees and rely on them to monitor compliance with rules. We could empower non-governmental organizations to monitor compliance or allow individuals to take federal departments to court when rules are broken. But political leaders have seen advantages in the watchdog model. Often, parliamentarians lack the knowledge and focus that are needed to perform oversight well. Appointing a watchdog is also a way of signalling seriousness about addressing a problem. And watchdogs act, in academic jargon, as a commitment device: they bind future governments to a policy because they are hard to eliminate. Weakening or eliminating a watchdog seems like abandoning the value that the watchdog protects.

Canada is not alone in appointing watchdogs. This has been a trend in many countries, with the exception of the United States. There are some scholars who believe that we are shifting to a new kind of "monitory democracy," in which the burden of scrutinizing governmental activities is relocated from legislators to independent "power-monitoring institutions." In fact, Canadian academics anticipated this shift forty years ago, describing it at that time as an important innovation in democratic rule.

Monitory democracy has a distinctive effect on politics within parliamentary systems. Canadian academics were quick to recognize this fact as well. Opposition politicians, eager for material with which to attack the governing party, readily seize on watchdog reports and give them more publicity. These reports also provide ready-made stories for journalists working on tight deadlines with modest resources. Every watchdog acquires a circle of organizations and individuals outside government who can be counted upon to promote and defend its work.

The surge of publicity that surrounds watchdog reports tends to encourage an exaggerated sense of the scale of a problem, as happened during the 2000 HRDC controversy. It also reinforces the belief that existing controls are inadequate and that the public service cannot be trusted to correct its behaviour. Controversies generate pressure for more controls so that the problem "never happens again." Auditors general themselves have worried about this dynamic. One of them, Kenneth Dye, warned in 1987: "I have become increasingly troubled that it is taken for granted that the appearance of the annual Report of the Auditor General is primarily an occasion that allows the media and the opposition parties in Parliament to lambast the government of the day; which, in turn, fuels the skepticism of many Canadians about government generally." Dye wrote this before the rise of social media and intensified party competition. The dynamic that he describes operates even more strongly today.

The overall effect of monitory democracy in a parliamentary system is to encourage a steady upward ratcheting of administrative controls. Political parties rarely make a detailed benefit–cost analysis when they promise new controls. Even if they do make a rough judgment about the benefits and costs of additional rules, they are liable to do this based on a misperception about the scale of the problem and with an eye on the immediate political advantages of action. Moreover, this rough analysis is not done on the margin, as economists would say. When they impose new rules, politicians do not consider the cumulative cost of all the controls already in place. And administrative controls are very hard to remove once they have been established, especially if a watchdog has been appointed to oversee them.

RISE OF THE POLITICAL SERVICE

Another form of control over the public service has been established in Ottawa since the 1980s. A 2015 report from the Public Policy Forum suggests we should call it the political service. The phrase is apt although not widely used. The political service consists of about six hundred political staff who are employed in the Prime Minister's Office (PMO) and offices of the nearly three dozen cabinet ministers. For comparison, the entire Department of Finance has about nine hundred employees.

We can think of the political service as a new institution, in the scholarly rather than the formal-legal sense. There is no law that names and regulates the political service, although perhaps there ought to be. Still, the political service clearly meets academic conceptions of an institution. This community has well-established boundaries: everyone knows who is within it and who is not. It also has a shared sense of identity, a distinctive culture, and well-defined ways of working.

The political service as an institution is relatively new. It has emerged over the last forty years. It would not have made sense to talk about a political service as an institution in the 1970s or early 1980s because political staffers were fewer in number, less well integrated as a group across ministries, and less important. Gordon Ritchie, a senior official at that time, recalls that he "barely knew the names of the political staff in the minister's office. The suggestion that my advice would pass through their censorship would have been offensive."

Members of the political service are often known as exempt staff because they are exempted from rules about hiring and firing that apply to the rest of the public service. (This is an unfortunate label because it emphasizes what political staff are not – career public servants – rather than what they are.) Ministers have discretion in deciding who they will hire, although the PMO may exercise influence on senior appointments within ministerial offices, and it controls the appointment of ministerial chiefs of staff. Political staff can be fired easily if ministers are unhappy with their work. They "are treated like race horses," a former staffer said in 2023, "where if you break a leg, they put a bullet in you ... They get rid of you. It's a different mentality than the rest of the outside world." Staff lose their jobs automatically when ministers are shuffled out of their post.

The political service started growing in the 1980s because overwhelmed ministers needed help in managing political work in Ottawa and in their constituencies. But there was another consideration too. The Conservative government that gained power in 1984 was suspicious of a public service that had been built up under long years of Liberal rule, and it increased the number of political staff to create a "countervailing" force. This justification is now invoked by both Liberal and Conservative governments. The political service is expected to perform "a challenge function with respect to public service advice" and ensure "greater responsiveness from public servants to ministerial direction."

The political service might be viewed as just another watchdog organization. It has distinctive features though. Political staff act on behalf of ministers who claim to represent the people through popular election. This is a much stronger claim to authority than can be made by any other watchdog. And this particular watchdog has plenary power. It is interested not only in transparency or the merit principle or fiscal discipline or sustainability but also in whatever ministers consider to be politically important.

Most watchdog bodies are comprised of workers who are highly skilled and experienced. This is not true of the political service. A 2006 study described the typical political staffer as "young, ambitious, and politically loyal … [but] often uneducated in the theory and operation of the machinery of government and regularly devoid of professional qualifications relevant to the ministries with which they are involved." In a 2018 assessment, professors Jennifer Robson and Paul Wilson agreed that "ministerial staffers are not as experienced as their public service interlocutors, and studies consistently point to the need for better training."

This particular watchdog body is also jittery. This is built into the culture of the political service. Michael Wernick, former head of the federal public service, observes that political staff in new governments are "pumped with adrenalin and a sense of having been proved right." Lack of job security means that staff are highly attentive to the needs of their minister. Political competition and a chaotic media environment add to the intensity of work. Political staff are "seized by a rapid response mentality." The objective is to defuse crises as quickly as possible, and this shapes interactions with the public service.

A code of conduct adopted in 2015 reminds political staff that they should treat public servants with respect and courtesy. In practice, though, political staff test the boundaries of propriety. An adviser to Prime Minister Stephen Harper conceded that political staff "did not hesitate to drive hundreds of people to the limits of their work ability every day." In a 2015 survey of deputy ministers, political staff were often described as "intrusive, obstructive, intimidating and rude." Pressure for quick responses was felt more intensely by deputy ministers in 2015 than in a similar survey fifteen years earlier. "I have middle managers who deal with the minister's office directly every day," a senior public servant said in 2023. "They can't direct public service but guess what? They do. The lines are blurry. They tell us what they want and how they want it."

The growth of the political service has had profound effects on the federal public service. Deputy ministers no longer have the unfettered access to ministers that they enjoyed before the 1980s, and their influence over policy decisions has declined. Senior political staff often act as gatekeepers, providing their own critique of departmental advice and sometimes blocking the flow of advice entirely.

Meanwhile, parts of the career public service have been infected by the same jitteriness that typifies the political service. Robson and Wilson observe that demands for help in fighting political brush fires may be delivered to career public servants at any hour of the day and any day of the week, with the expectation of an immediate response. The frequency and unpredictability of these interventions raises stress within government offices and undermines the capacity to follow work plans.

It also changes the mood in government offices. "There's a short-termism and unpredictability in people's lives," one senior official told Robson and Wilson. "The personality of the institution starts to shift so that even when it gets breaks from some of that pressure it may not be hardwired to do some of that longer-term analysis." A 2011 report from the Public Service Commission shared concern about "the over-responsiveness of public servants to the priorities of the government-of-the-day and a growing role for public servants in tailoring and communicating public messages."

There is good evidence that stronger oversight from the political service has induced caution within the public service. Senior officials are more hesitant about providing policy advice that seems likely to antagonize political staff. This tendency has been observed over two decades, in both Liberal and Conservative governments. Public servants at lower levels are also more careful about decisions that might erupt into controversy. Political staff want a "no surprises environment" for their ministers. Public servants respond by sticking to protocol. "There's a huge amount of self-policing," one civil servant said in a 2016 study, "because you never know when you're going to get in trouble."

DECLINE OF INDEPENDENT REVIEW

Over the span of a half-century, and especially over the last thirty years, administrative and political controls on the federal public service have become more complex and burdensome. The expansion of these controls is itself evidence of adaptation within the system. Controls have been extended as our ideas about good government have evolved and also as parties have struggled to win power and preserve public trust in federal authority within a more complicated political environment.

But adaptations often have unintended consequences, and evidence is mounting about the side effects of intensified administrative and political control. One of these side effects is increased compliance costs. We do not know exactly what it costs for departments and agencies to meet the expectations of watchdogs and political overseers, and to maintain the watchdogs and overseers themselves, and how this cost compares to the benefits of intensified control. It is likely, though, that these compliance costs are substantial. Some costs can be expressed easily in dollar terms; others are less tangible, such as declining capacity of departments to move nimbly in pursuit of departmental objectives, declining ability to make and execute long-term plans, and reluctance to experiment and offer frank advice.

An accretion of controls is not the only challenge facing the federal public service today. At the start of the chapter, I also noted how the shift toward platform governance has created confusion about the policy role of the public service. Increasingly, promises are made by party leaders before public servants are able to give advice about the feasibility of delivering on those promises.

Added to this is disruption within the public service caused by the COVID pandemic. During the pandemic, many public servants began working from home. The practice of working remotely has continued on a large scale within the federal public service after the pandemic. This unplanned experiment seems to promise a major gain in workplace productivity. Civil servants spend less time and money on commuting, while departments economize on office space.

But our knowledge about the benefits and costs of remote work is still limited. When we think about productivity, we look first at more obvious and immediate aspects of work, such as processing cases or holding meetings. We know less about the longer-term and less-tangible effects of remote work. For example, what is likely to happen to agency performance in the longer run if employees no longer engage informally at the workplace? And what effect will remote work have on the transmission of organizational culture, that set of shared understandings about organizational goals and fundamental values such as political neutrality and respect for the law? A December 2023 report on the federal public service observed that the shift to "hybrid work environments" meant that there were "fewer conventional opportunities for ongoing dialogue on the core values and ethics of the institution."

There is yet another challenge likely to face the federal public service in the near future: retrenchment. The service has grown by almost 40 per cent since the Trudeau government came to power in 2015, from 257,000 to 357,000 people. More growth is projected in coming years. The last time that the federal bureaucracy expanded this quickly was in the 1970s, a half-century ago. Some effort at restraint or downsizing seems inevitable. It may be set in motion by a change in government or by an economic downturn that pinches federal revenues. In either case, pressure to downsize may come quickly, and cuts may be poorly planned. In the past, downsizing efforts resulted in a reduction of staff responsible for forward-thinking, as I noted in chapter 3.

Given all the challenges facing the federal public service, there is a compelling argument for a thorough and independent review of its role and structure. In the twentieth century, there was a frequently used device for executing such reviews: the royal commission. The federal government established six commissions to examine the federal service between 1912 and 1979.

The most extensive of these reviews was conducted by the Glassco Commission on Government Organization. Set up by the Conservative government of John Diefenbaker in 1960, the commission was a "grand inquest," in the words of professor J.E. Hodgetts. It hired a temporary staff of two hundred and organized more than twenty study teams before delivering its final report in 1963. The report's theme resonates today. The commission found a lack of "systemic flexibility" within the public service, which it attributed to a fixation with administrative controls. Many of the commission's recommendations were adopted over the next decade. One observer has described the Glassco report as a "revolutionary milestone" in the history of Canadian public administration.

As we saw in chapter 3, royal commissions have fallen out of favour in Canada, except for those that investigate wrongdoing and failures in government. The last royal commission charged with reviewing the condition of the public service finished its work more than forty years ago. Since then, reform in the public service has proceeded in different ways. Periodically, an emergency, fiscal crisis, or scandal leads to restructuring somewhere in the public service. Central agencies have also launched reviews about the administration of particular laws that have sometimes led to reform of the laws themselves. And since the 1990s, clerks of the privy council have also launched their own exercises to revitalize the federal bureaucracy. The most recent is a 2023 effort by clerk John Hannaford to organize "a broad conversation" among public servants about values and ethics "within a dynamic and increasingly complex environment."

All these approaches to reform are useful, to a point. Episodic reviews of particular laws are no substitute for an examination of the role and structure of the public service as a whole. Larger questions about the purpose of the public service are neglected within such reviews. Similarly, the cumulative effect of many laws is overlooked. And some topics have remained off limits: governments have avoided scrutiny of the expanding political service. There also limits to what privy council clerks can accomplish in their own reform exercises. Senior public servants are busy people, preoccupied with the day-to-day work of government. They face constraints on what they can do and say publicly. And because they are government employees, anything that they might say in defence of the public service is likely to be viewed skeptically by legislators and citizens.

Today, we need something bigger: a thoughtful conversation about how we design the federal establishment so that it can function well for the next generation of Canadians. This means a review not just of the career public service but also the political service. As I argue in the next chapter, the time is past due for another independent inquiry with the scale and ambition of the Glassco Commission.

7 Canada: Preserving Adaptability

In this book, I have made five claims. The first is that adaptability matters. When we look at any political system, one of the most important questions we should ask is whether it has the capacity to reinvent itself to accommodate new conditions. Adaptability matters because there is no fixed or universal formula for governing that works in all places and for all time. Grand strategy, that set of generally shared understandings about national aspirations and how to achieve them, must be revised frequently. Institutions and practices, the means by which strategy is converted into action, must be overhauled as well.

This work of state renovation never ends. Any political system that cannot keep up with the work of renovation will find itself increasingly at odds with the world. Manageable problems will turn into unmanageable crises. Crises will feed on one another, overwhelming the capacity of leaders to respond effectively. The result will be some form of state collapse. This is not a rare phenomenon. Most countries in the world are counted as fragile, which is another way of saying they are uncomfortably close to collapse.

My second claim has to do with the prerequisites for adaptability. I have argued that an adaptable political system must be capable of performing four functions. The system must anticipate potential dangers.

It must be capable of devising grand strategies likely to be effective in addressing the whole set of anticipated dangers. It must be capable of building an adequate level of support among politically influential groups, and the public at large, for one grand strategy or another. And it must be capable of restructuring institutions and practices so that they can perform the tasks required by the new grand strategy.

My third claim relates to the adaptability of a certain kind of political system, what I have called the federal-liberal-democratic (FLD) model of government. Arguments have been advanced about the superior adaptability of FLD systems when compared to technocratic-authoritarian systems like China. But the case for FLD systems is not open-and-shut. There is good evidence that adaptability might be undermined within FLD systems because of their tendency toward short-sightedness, gridlock, and miscoordination. And we should avoid generalizations about FLD systems. They vary in terms of institutional design, practices, and culture, and these differences have an important influence on adaptability.

My fourth claim has to do with the adaptability of one particular FLD system at one moment in time: Canada, in the middle-to-late twentieth century. To be clear, we should not be sentimental about Canada in that era. Most Canadians in that time were worse off than most Canadians today. Still, the system in that era had distinctive features that enhanced adaptability, allowing the country to survive and improve itself. People invested in forward-thinking, worked hard at building agreement among leaders and citizens, and constructed bureaucracies that were professional, honest, and efficient.

My fifth and final claim has to do with governance in Canada today. Institutions, practices, and culture have changed – often for the better, sometimes for the worse. Short-sightedness, a chronic weakness of democratic systems, appears to be resurgent in Canada. The capacity of the system to think about grand strategy for the next generation has been reduced. Routines that once helped to build common understanding among national leaders have been abandoned. The Canadian public sphere, which is an engine for producing common understanding within the entire population, is in trouble. The federal public service, a single but important part of Canada's bureaucratic machinery, seems less nimble than it once was.

How did Canada arrive at this state of affairs? Partly it is the unintended consequence of successful adaptation in the past. Canada is a more populous and diverse country than it was a couple of generations ago. Political power has also been redistributed: among orders and branches of government, between governments and citizens, and between governments and markets. By and large, these changes should be celebrated. But the end result is that the Canadian political system is now much more complex. It has more parts, all moving faster.

This means that the problem of coordination within the system is bigger than it used to be. We cannot take for granted that everyone in the system has a clear understanding of what everyone else is trying to accomplish, or that everyone is trying, so far as they can, to move in the same direction. In chapter 2, I introduced the notion of an adaptability trap, a condition in which a system reinvents itself in positive ways but finds that it has inadvertently compromised its capacity for more reinvention. Canada may have moved closer to an adaptability trap over the last forty years.

Of course, there is more to the story. Canada has also been affected by what economists like to call exogenous shocks – big changes beyond the control of Canadian governments. The most obvious shock is the rapid transformation in information and communication technologies since the early 1990s. Another is globalization. These two changes have also made Canadian politics more complicated and frenetic.

There is a third, critical explanation of why adaptability in Canada has declined: inaction by governments. Falling into an adaptability trap is not inevitable. It happens when leaders do not think carefully about what must be done to hold a system together, and preserve adaptability, as it becomes bigger and more complex. Similarly, leaders ought to think carefully about the effect of exogenous shocks on cohesion and adaptability within the system and take the appropriate compensatory measures.

So far in this century, Canadian leaders have not engaged in enough of this system-level thinking. Worse still, they have dismantled some mechanisms that once contributed to adaptability. Why have leaders done this? Maybe they have been distracted by the relentless pressures of day-to-day politics. Or maybe they are still suffering a hangover from the neo-liberal '90s, when many people thought that the world had reached the end of history and the future would be uneventful.

The good news is that Canada is on the edge of an adaptability trap, not in one. Canada remains one of the best-governed countries in the world today. And there are many steps that can be taken to improve adaptability. Below, I describe some possible reforms. These reforms are affordable and easily implemented. None require painful constitutional change. These reforms would accomplish several goals. They would provide a counterbalance to short-termism, by encouraging attention to national strategy for the long term. They would stabilize the national political conversation, so that leaders and citizens are focused on a common agenda. And they would raise the quality of dialogue, by increasing knowledge and promoting civility. More broadly, these reforms would improve the prospects for reaching agreement on the path forward for Canada and for translating plans into action.

NEW INVESTMENTS IN FORWARD-THINKING

An important first step is to reinvest in forward-thinking. A decade ago, Mel Cappe, a former head of the Canadian public service, offered a suggestion about how to do this. Lamenting "the absence of a big-ideas, priorities agenda for Canada," Cappe proposed the creation of a "royal commission on the economic, social, cultural, environmental and international prospects of Canada." He envisaged an inquiry on the model of the Macdonald Commission of the 1980s, the Gordon Commission of the 1950s, and the Rowell-Sirois Commission of the 1930s. Such a commission would be independent and politically balanced. It would have a budget for research and a mandate to promote a national conversation about long-term challenges.

Three objections are usually made against a proposal such as this, but none carry much weight. The first is expense. This is a distraction. In today's dollars, the cost of the Macdonald Commission of the 1980s was about $65 million. That is less than what Parliament spends on the CBC every three weeks. It is less than half of what the federal government spent on advertising in 2022. It is one-ninth of what the Trudeau government spent to host the 2018 G7 summit in La Malbaie, Quebec.

The second objection is that commissions take too long to produce recommendations and that these recommendations are sometimes unworkable. The mistake here is to think of royal commissions simply as machines for producing recommendations. As I observed in chapter 2, policy prescriptions are only one of the outputs of a royal commission and not even the most important of these outputs. We can imagine a royal commission that avoids exact recommendations and defines options instead. Emphasizing options rather than recommendations would also dispense with the third objection, usually raised by ministers and their staff, which is that recommendations tend to box governments in.

The main value of a royal commission is that it focuses the country's attention and stabilizes the agenda for political debate. A commission would provide a strong signal about what matters, and it would maintain that signal for two or three years. By sponsoring research, the commission would concentrate attention within the academic community. By organizing hearings and publishing reports, the commission would concentrate attention among journalists, interest groups, and legislators. A commission would promote a common understanding about the facts, even if Canadians disagree on how to respond to those facts. A twenty-first-century commission could use digital innovations for public engagement and education that were unavailable to its predecessors.

Skeptics might argue that a royal commission is unlikely to have broad legitimacy because parties have grown too far apart: if one party likes its work, another will not. These skeptics might be right, although we should be reluctant to accept the hypothesis without testing it, by attempting to construct a royal commission that does have cross-party support.

There is a second way to invest in forward-thinking that works even when parties are sharply divided. Many European governments have created party foundations, with the goal of improving the quality of policy-making, encouraging a long-term perspective, and promoting civic engagement. In Germany there are six of these foundations, each one allied with a national political party. These foundations are publicly funded, based on a formula that links the amount of support to a party's success in recent elections. Although foundations are affiliated with parties, they are not directly controlled by party leaders, and they are strictly barred from participating in party campaigning.

Germany's foundations are a well-established part of the country's political system. These foundations see themselves as think-tanks and educators. One describes itself as "an early warning and reconnaissance system" that invents new ideas for responding to long-term trends and "exploring potential support for these in different milieus of society." German party foundations run programs to raise public understanding of the political process and major issues, and to encourage citizen engagement in politics. They promote education of young people through scholarship programs and maintain party archives as well. As a 1981 statement issued jointly by German party foundations explained, all this work sustains the political culture that is essential to survival of any liberal democracy. Party foundations "vitalize and stabilize" the German political system.

The idea of establishing party foundations in Canada is not new. It was recommended in 1991 by the Royal Commission on Electoral Reform – the Lortie Commission – for two reasons. The first was that Canadian parties no longer played the role in political education that they had earlier in the twentieth century. The second was that parties were clearly lacking in the capacity to develop policy, especially on long-term questions.

The case for party foundations in Canada is even more compelling today than it was in 1991. While the educational role of parties has shrunk further, their policy role has increased. As I said in chapter 3, party platforms have become more important documents, but parties lack the capacity to draft platforms that are well-reasoned and grounded in a broader perspective. Foundations would improve the ability of parties to develop grand strategies that are thoughtful, anchored in research, and attentive to the long run. Moreover, foundations could build public understanding and support for these strategies through their educative role.

As with royal commissions, expense should not be a concern. If Canada had party foundations that were funded at the same level as Germany's, accounting for population differences, the cost would be about $75 million a year. By contrast, the cost of administering a federal election is more than $500 million.

REVIVING DIALOGUE AMONG CANADA'S LEADERS

Complete consensus among leaders within a decentralized political system is unattainable. But that does not mean the effort to build consensus is pointless. Within a decentralized political system, misunderstandings and disagreements can have fatal consequences, for individuals (as Canadians saw during the COVID pandemic) and for the system as a whole. A decentralized system requires mechanisms for reducing misunderstandings and disagreements so far as possible, or, put more positively, for promoting a common understanding about national challenges and how they will be managed. In the twentieth century, one of those mechanisms was summitry, in the form of regular first ministers' conferences.

Summitry ought to be revived in Canada, in the form of an annual meeting that includes all first ministers as well as leaders of national Indigenous organizations. This would be a proper meeting, not just a dinner or PowerPoint presentation. It would have an element of formality and ritual. The meeting would be at least one day and perhaps two, based on a format that remains consistent from year to year. Discussion would follow a commonly agreed-upon agenda, made public beforehand. Leaders would meet behind closed doors, but they would agree on a summary of discussion that would be released publicly afterward.

The purpose of the meeting would be discussion, not dealmaking. First ministers and Indigenous leaders can meet at other times to hammer out agreements on new policies. The annual summit would be held even when no new policies were proposed, and the lack of any formal agreement on policy at the end of the summit would not be construed as a sign of failure. In other words, the same norms would be applied to domestic summits as are applied to international summits like meetings of G7 leaders.

The idea of an annual summit of Canadian leaders is hardly new. As we saw in chapter 4, regular summits were recommended by the Rowell-Sirois Commission more than eighty years ago, and the idea has been endorsed by political scientists many times since then. Stefan Dupré made the case for "routinized federal-provincial summitry" in 1988, suggesting that regular meetings would encourage "constructive patterns of behavior." Richard Simeon and Martin Papillon suggested in 2004 that routinized summits would also eliminate arguments about the need for a meeting and who deserves a seat at the table. Hamish Telford argued in 2008 that regular summits would promote the growth of "trust ties" among national leaders.

In addition, summitry performs symbolic functions. A summit that is held regularly and conducted with some formality conveys a message that leaders are committed to the Canadian federation. A summit that includes Indigenous leaders, without haggling about their right to participate, conveys a message about the inclusive character of that federation. The elements of summitry – a publicly accessible agenda, in camera conversation, a communiqué afterward – all convey the message that civil deliberation is possible even when participants have deep disagreements.

Perhaps more important, from the point of view of adaptability, is the role that summits can play in providing focus for political debate more broadly. A publicly accessible agenda would not just provide structure for the summit itself. It would also help to focus and stabilize the national conversation about public policy. Other groups and individuals (such as legislative committees, advocacy groups, and academics) would orient their work to address problems that are given priority at the summit. This has been the experience with international summits.

The Council of the Federation ought to be reconfigured so that it can act as a secretariat for this annual summit, as well as other meetings. The council's head might perform the diplomatic roles of negotiating the agenda and moderating the summit, and council staff might even have a role in producing research tied to that agenda, just as other secretariats already do. The council could still play a role in organizing annual meetings for premiers, and it could support other meetings of ministers as well. In fact, it would be useful to consider whether similar work currently done by other organizations, such as the Canadian Intergovernmental Conference Secretariat, should be consolidated within a restructured Council of the Federation. There may be administrative efficiencies that result from combined operations. However, efficiencies are not the main point. The Council of the Federation ought to be restructured so that it lives up to its name. And national leaders ought to meet regularly because that is what allies do.

REPAIRING THE PUBLIC SPHERE

Adaptability can also be improved by repairing the Canadian public sphere, that space within which Canadians engage in debate about the country's future. A healthy public sphere is critical to adaptability for several reasons: it unleashes the problem-solving capacity of citizens and non-governmental organizations, deepens public understanding and support for government policies, and promotes the sort of common understanding that facilitates coordinated action in a decentralized system. In several ways, the public sphere performs the same role as summits, except on a much larger scale.

As I said in chapter 5, the Canadian public sphere is not in good health. It has suffered because of technological shocks and governmental neglect. The boundaries of the public sphere have eroded, so that Canadians wield less influence over the direction of their national conversation. The agenda has been destabilized, so that the national conversation is harder to follow. Norms about civility and open-mindedness have been strained. The quality of conversation is compromised by low levels of knowledge about history, government, and policy challenges.

What can be done about this? The first step is simply to name the problem properly. Too often, initiatives that are aimed at restoring the quality of the national conversation have been mislabelled as arts-and-culture policies. Of course, arts and culture are important, but the problem we are concerned with is different and more fundamental. It relates to the capacity of a community – Canada as a whole – to have a constructive conversation about looming challenges and how to address them.

Admittedly, politicians are unlikely to talk about the health of the public sphere. The phrase is too academic. Clever politicians must find some alternative language. In a general sense, it is about protecting Canadian democracy and the capacity for self-determination. A 2018 report from Public Policy Forum talked about protecting "informed democratic discourse." Conservatives have talked about preserving the "Canadian public conversation."

The next step is for friends of the public sphere to retrieve the populist mantle. We must reject the notion that governmental intervention in the marketplace of ideas is necessarily an assault on freedom. There is no liberal democracy anywhere in which government has not acted at some point to protect the public sphere. Even in the United States, there is a long tradition of government intervention to assure a national conversation on public affairs. Well-designed interventions have the capacity to enhance freedom, in the sense that they enable citizens to make meaningful choices about development of their country. Such measures "give Canadians back control of their lives," to borrow populist language.

The federal bureaucracy ought to be reorganized to reflect a new emphasis on protecting the public sphere. As I said in chapter 2, one of the virtues of the Canadian system is that prime ministers have more freedom to undertake such reorganizations. One obvious step is restructuring the Department of Canadian Heritage so that democracy promotion is recognized as a key part of its mission. The department ought to be renamed accordingly. There is precedent: Canada has already had ministers for democratic reform (in 2003–05 and again in 2006–15), democratic renewal (2005–06), and democratic institutions (2015–19), although these ministers have not been supported by similarly named departments or agencies. Sweden has a minister for democracy, and Britain's opposition Labour Party has a shadow minister for democracy. In Canada, a new "Department for Democracy and Heritage," which might also include programs presently located in other departments and agencies, would give more clarity of purpose and coherence to federal programs relating to the public sphere.

This may also be a good time to consider reviving one of Canada's long-defunct advisory councils, in modified form. The Science Council of Canada was established in 1966 and abolished twenty-five years later as a cost-saving measure. Its mission was to engage in long-term thinking and provide counsel to governments on science and technology issues. Many scientists condemned the decision to close the council in 1992, and there have been many calls for its revival in light of the revolutions in science and technology since that time. A 2018 study concluded: "The need has never been greater." A new "Council on Technology and Society" could play a valuable role in providing policy-makers and citizens with credible advice about the social and economic impact of emerging technologies such as artificial intelligence.

HEALTH CHECK FOR THE PUBLIC AND POLITICAL SERVICES

Public servants at all levels of government make an important contribution to adaptability. Sometimes they do this by offering policy advice or building agreement among stakeholders about proposed policies. Primarily, though, they contribute to adaptability by translating new policies into action. As I said in chapter 6, the capacity of the federal public service to perform this task appears to be compromised.

I have described the main problem confronting the federal public service: a decades-long accretion of administrative and political controls. Controls are usually imposed with good intentions. However, governments have not always weighed benefits and costs properly when controls have been introduced, and for a very long time, there has been no assessment of the cumulative costs of controls. Some of these costs are easily calculated, while others are less tangible, such as a decline in innovation and risk-taking, and decay in the quality of policy advice.

If we were talking about controls on private businesses, rather than controls on federal departments, we would describe this as a problem of regulatory burden. Reducing regulatory burden in the private sector has been a priority of many Western governments for a long time. The Organisation for Economic Co-operation and Development, an international body that counts Canada as a member, says there is consensus among governments that "national regulatory systems require periodic maintenance": "One of the most important tasks facing governments today is updating of the accumulated regulations and formalities that have gone unexamined over years or decades … Periodic and systematic review of existing regulations is needed to ensure that outcomes are assessed, unneeded or inefficient rules are weeded out, and needed rules are adapted to new economic and social conditions."

This logic applies with equal force to regulation within the federal public service. Periodic and systematic review is required in this context too. In chapter 6, I also noted other reasons for an overall review, including the need to think about the impact of remote work and the prospect of austerity-driven restructuring in coming years.

But if there is an overall review, how should it be structured? In 2022, professor Donald Savoie recommended the establishment of a royal commission on the federal public service. The federal public service is a troubled institution, Savoie said, and "nobody knows what to do about it." A royal commission seemed to him to be the best way of encouraging "sober second thought" about its purpose and design.

Not everyone agrees on the need for a royal commission. Former public service head Michael Wernick acknowledged in 2023 that

"Canada has allowed its supply chain of idea generation and debate about its public sector to erode to a pitiful state." But Wernick doubted the usefulness of a royal commission and proposed more "practical measures," such as an advisory council on the public service appointed by the prime minister and a fund to promote research on the public service managed by central agencies. A trio of respected public administration professors have also acknowledged the need for a "rethink of the direction of the public service." But this trio thought that the royal commission model was outmoded and also recommended initiatives within the public service to promote institutional learning on a routine basis.

The difficulty with these alternative proposals is that they are unlikely to address the hardest questions facing the federal public service and would lack credibility if they tried to address those questions. For example, any review exercise that is directly controlled by the prime minister or other ministers is unlikely to take a hard look at the role of the political service. And even if such a review did reach conclusions on the role of the political service, those findings would be dismissed by outside observers. Similarly, any critique of administrative controls that comes out of a review led by public servants will be viewed as special pleading, just as we view business complaints about over-regulation as special pleading. The only way to obtain a comprehensive and credible assessment of the public service is by giving the task to an independent body.

The last royal commission that was charged with studying the federal public service was appointed in 1976. That was before the arrival of personal computers, the Internet, the political service, and the broad devolution of power to other governments, businesses, and citizens in the late twentieth century. Another review, almost a half-century later, is hardly excessive. A royal commission on the role of Canada's public and political services would provide a road map for evolution of these two institutions over the next thirty years.

DANGERS AHEAD

What will happen if these reforms, or reforms like them, are not adopted and adaptability within the Canadian system atrophies as a result? The system as a whole will become more crisis prone. Small problems will mushroom into big problems and feed on one another. Leaders and their advisers will find more work on their desks than they can handle competently. Relations between national leaders will become more rancorous, and citizens will become more frustrated. Compliance with laws will decline, while protests increase. Eventually, the system will be overwhelmed and it will collapse. Canada will break into several smaller and weaker systems, or it will be absorbed into a larger system.

This may seem like a dark view of the future. A realist would reply that this is the eventual fate of all political systems. We should not make the mistake of taking the durability of any political system, including Canada's, for granted. Vigilance and preparedness are important because things can get out of hand quickly. Look at the symptoms enumerated in the previous paragraph and think about the realities of Canadian politics today. The warning lights are flickering already. It would be reckless to delay action until they are burning steadily.

Vigilance and preparedness are especially important now because the remaining decades of this century will be treacherous. We can reasonably expect to see:

- *dramatic disruptions in climate*, including frequent emergencies that consume our attention and collective resources

- *massive migration* that is triggered by climate change, which will test the capacity of states to control borders and govern their territory

- *growing political instability* within four major polities (the United States, the European Union, India, and China) that is induced by climate change and other factors

- *intensified competition* among states for access to water, habitable land, and other resources that lie within Canadian borders
- *resurgence of interstate warfare*, after an unusually long period of peace, that is aggravated by a technological revolution in weaponry
- *economic dislocation* caused by the arrival of artificial intelligence, robotics, and other advanced technologies
- *challenges of integration* within Canada that are associated with the planned arrival of fifteen million immigrants, and the unplanned arrival of many more, over the next thirty years

Of course, Canada will not be alone in confronting such challenges. Some countries will respond to them better than others. One potential danger is that countries will shift away from democracy toward authoritarianism as their problems deepen. Centralized or strongman rule may seem like the only way of regaining control over events. This was the global experience in the 1920s and 1930s, and we are seeing evidence today of a similar shift toward authoritarianism, described by one expert as a "democratic recession." Much of the progress on human rights that the world has witnessed over the last century could be undone if this trend continues. Even so, citizens in many countries might be prepared to sacrifice human rights if they believe that authoritarianism is the only way of keeping safe in a dangerous world.

The remainder of this century will be a contest between democracies and authoritarian systems or alternately between open and closed societies. The central question will be which form of government is better at adapting to rapidly changing conditions. Chinese leaders already have an opinion on this question. President Xi Jinping claimed in 2023 that the Chinese system has the advantage over Western systems because it is "forward-looking," follows "the principle of strategy," and is able to make plans that are "adhered to for a long time."

Our assignment is to prove that a trade-off between openness and adaptability is not necessary – that a highly decentralized system, designed to respect individual freedom and community rights, can also respond nimbly to looming dangers.

Acknowledgments

I am grateful to Taki Sarantakis, president of the Canada School of Public Service, for the opportunity to serve as the Jocelyne Bourgon Visiting Scholar in 2022–23, and to Josianne Paul and Genevieve Nappert-Cazeault of CSPS for their assistance during the year. Thanks also to Emily Andrew, senior editor at McGill-Queen's University Press, for her enthusiastic support of this book project, to Shelagh Plunkett and Eleanor Gasparik for their thoughtful copyediting, and to Alexandra Peace for indexing. While writing this book, I benefited from conversations with a large number of people working in and around government and from the comments of several readers of draft manuscripts. Their generosity with time and candour is much appreciated. Finally, I would like to remember scholarly colleagues who have passed away in recent years, including friends from my years at the School of Policy Studies at Queen's University, whose work has influenced these pages, and also to recognize a new generation of Canadian scholars in public policy and administration whose research has been equally influential.

Notes

Preface

vii "Young Canadians Express Real Fears": Leger Marketing, *2023 Youth Study Report* (Leger Marketing, 2022).

Chapter One

3 lifespan of empires: Rein Taagepera, "Expansion and Contraction Patterns of Large Polities," *International Studies Quarterly* 41, no. 3 (1997): 475–504.

4 Most states are also unstable: Fund for Peace, *Fragile States Index Annual Report* (Fund for Peace, 2023), 6–7.

4 devise a grand strategy: For further discussion of my approach to strategy, see *Strategies for Governing: Reinventing Public Administration for a Dangerous Century* (Cornell University Press, 2019). In that book, I use the phrase "governing strategy." For convenience, I use the more familiar phrase "grand strategy" here. Grand strategy in this context covers both foreign and domestic policy.

5 Machiavelli describes a world: *The Essential Writings of Machiavelli* (Modern Library, 2007), 94, 130, 253.

6 "Everything on earth": Cary Baynes and Richard Wilhelm, *The I Ching* (Routledge & Kegan Paul, 1951), 50–1.

6 "be mindful of danger": Jinping Xi, *The Governance of China* (Foreign Languages Press, 2014), 304.

6 "seemingly unlimited": Peter Ryckmans, "The Chinese Attitude toward the Past," *China Heritage Quarterly* 14 (2008), http://www.chinaheritage quarterly.org/articles.php?searchterm=014_chineseAttitude.inc& issue=014.

6 "dynamic social systems": Roxanne Dunbar-Ortiz, *An Indigenous Peoples' History of the United States* (Beacon Press, 2014), 79.

6 "stunning ability": Pekka Hämäläinen, *Lakota America: A New History of Indigenous Power* (Yale University Press, 2019), 9.

7 "experimental process": John Dewey, *The Public and Its Problems* (Holt, 1927), 34.

7 "a final perfected form": Robert MacIver, *The Modern State* (Clarendon Press, 1926), vii.

7 "stable state": Donald A. Schön, *Beyond the Stable State* (Norton, 1973), 30.

7 "The challenge of adapting government": Donald Kettl, *Escaping Jurassic Government* (Brookings Institution, 2016), 180.

8 "reared for immortality": William Story, *Life and Letters* (Little, Brown and Company, 1851), 139.

8 "Newtonian theory": Woodrow Wilson, *Constitutional Government in the United States* (Columbia University Press, 1908), 54–6.

8 "Study government": John Adams, *The Works of John Adams* (Little, Brown and Company, 1851), 6:481.

8 "last a thousand years": Pierre Trudeau, "Canada in Weaklings' Hands," *Montreal Gazette*, 28 May 1987, A4.

8 "finally resolve": Peter Morton and Alan Toulin, "New Economic Order on the Table," *Financial Post*, 25 September 1991, 1.

8 "golden straitjacket": Thomas Friedman, *The Lexus and the Olive Tree* (Farrar, Straus and Giroux, 1999), 104.

9 "the end of history": Francis Fukuyama, "The End of History?," *National Interest* 16, no. 3 (1989): 3–16.

9 "final form": John Gray, *Black Mass: Apocalyptic Religion and the Death of Utopia* (Farrar, Straus and Giroux, 2007), 29, 124.

11 "renewal of every aspect": Mikhail Gorbachev, *Perestroika: New Thinking for Our Country and the World* (Harper & Row, 1987), 17, 35.

11 not the same as crisis management: Arjen Boin, *The Politics of Crisis Management* (Cambridge University Press, 2005), 2.

11 Resilience has been defined: Andrew Zolli and Ann Marie Healy, *Resilience: Why Things Bounce Back* (Free Press, 2012), 6.

15 John Dewey and Karl Popper: Dewey, *The Public and Its Problems*; Karl Popper, *The Open Society and Its Enemies* (Routledge, 1945).

16 the strategy is *emergent*: Ionut Popescu, *Emergent Strategy and Grand Strategy* (Johns Hopkins University Press, 2017).

17 "irrational exuberance": Federal Reserve Chairman Alan Greenspan, quoted in "Fed Chief's Comments Shake Up Markets," *The Atlanta Journal*, 6 December 1996, 1.

18 "thirst for enemies": Friedrich Nietzsche, *On the Genealogy of Morals* (Oxford University Press, 2008), 29.

18 many political psychologists agreed: Vamik Volkan, *The Need to Have Enemies and Allies* (Aronson, 1988).

18 "progressive loss": Jonathan Rauch, "Demosclerosis," *National Journal* (1992): 1998–2003.

19 "inherent foe": Harold Laski, "The Obsolescence of Federalism," *New Republic* 98 (1939): 367–9, 369.

19 "interwoven administration": Kettl, *Escaping Jurassic Government*, 54.

Chapter Two

23 "sister countries": For this and other phrases in this paragraph, search the Web for examples.

24 "savage grip": The phrase is Louis Hémon's, from his novel *Maria Chapdelaine* (Macmillan, 1922), 184.

24 "taking the national pulse": Margaret Atwood, *Survival: A Thematic Guide to Canadian Literature* (House of Anansi, 1972), 27–8.

25 overriding concern: H. Neatby, *William Lyon Mackenzie King*, volume III, 1932–39 (University of Toronto Press, 1976), epilogue.

25 "most passionate interest": Lester B. Pearson, *Mike: The Memoirs of the Rt. Hon. Lester B. Pearson* (University of Toronto Press, 2015), 3:236.

25 "take Canada for granted": Terrance Wills, "PM for 'Change without Revolution,'" *Montreal Gazette*, 30 November 1995, 1.

25 "the end of Canada": George Grant, *Lament for a Nation* (McGill-Queen's University Press, 2005), 4.

25 "helpless": Frank Underhill, "The Sirois Commission as Historians," *The Canadian Forum* (1940): 234.

25 "distintegration of Canada": Neatby, *William Lyon Mackenzie King*, chapter 11.

25 "surrender of sovereignty": Maude Barlow, *Parcel of Rogues* (Key Porter Books, 1990).

25 "the old sweeping issues": Commencement Address at Yale University, 11 June 1962.

26 "so little internal crisis": State of the Union Address, 27 January 2000.

26 complacency about its future: Thomas D'Aquino, *Private Power, Public Purpose* (Signal, 2023), 304.

26 "an inquiring people": David E. Smith, "Bagehot, the Crown and the Canadian Constitution," *Canadian Journal of Political Science* 28, no. 4 (1995): 619–35, 626.

26 two types of commissions: Gregory Inwood and Carolyn Johns, *Commissions of Inquiry and Policy Change* (University of Toronto Press, 2014), 13–15.

27 "staff of experts": J.W. Dafoe, "The Canadian Federal System Under Review," *Foreign Affairs* 18, no. 4 (1940): 646–58.

27 "most exhaustive investigation": Donald V. Smiley, *The Rowell-Sirois Report* (McClelland and Stewart, 1967), 1–6.

27 "the kind of world": Underhill, "The Sirois Commission as Historians," 235.

27 "all the average man": "Briefly," *Windsor Daily Star*, 26 October 1940, 2.

27 "balanced framework": Simon Kuznets, "Canada's Economic Prospects," *American Economic Review* 49, no. 3 (1959): 359–85, 383.

28 "a landmark": R.A. Musgrave, "The Carter Commission Report," *The Canadian Journal of Economics* 1, no. 1 (1968): 159–82, 159, 182.

28 "where Canadians were going": David Laidler and William Robson, *Prospects for Canada: Progress and Challenges 20 Years after the Macdonald Commission* (Renouf Publishing, 2005), 6.

28 "marked, if not inspired": Nicholas D'Ombrain, "Public Inquiries in Canada," *Canadian Public Administration* 40, no. 1 (1997): 86–107, 87.

28 "storefront of ideas": Mackenzie Valley Pipeline Inquiry, *Northern Frontier, Northern Homeland* (J. Lorimer, 1977), 2:223.

29 "contemplate the future": R.W. Phidd, "The Economic Council of Canada," *Canadian Public Administration* 18, no. 3 (1975): 428–73, 433–4.

29 largest think tank: Laurent Dobuzinskis, "Back to the Future: Is There a Case for Re-Establishing the Economic Council or the Science Council?" (paper, Annual Meeting of the Canadian Political Science Association, Winnipeg, 3 June 2004), 6.

29 "an overall view": Martin L. Friedland, *My Life in Crime and Other Academic Adventures* (University of Toronto Press, 2007), 168.

29 "long-term research": Monique Jérome-Forget, "Institute for Research on Public Policy," in *Think Tanks and Civil Societies*, ed. Kent Weaver (Transaction Publishers, 2000), 87.

29 "Public sphere": Jürgen Habermas, "The Public Sphere," *New German Critique*, no. 3 (1974): 49–55. While this book was proceeding to production, Habermas published a short volume about the effects of new media on the public sphere, which advances arguments similar to those in this chapter: *A New Structural Transformation of the Public Sphere and Deliberative Politics* (Polity, 2023).

29 "shared public space": Elihu Katz, "And Deliver Us from Segmentation," *Annals of the American Academy of Political and Social Science* 546, no. 1 (1996): 22–33.

30 "Too often our convictions": *The Canadian Forum*, October 1920, 3.

30 "modern means of communication": Robert MacIver, *The Web of Government* (Macmillan, 1947), 221–2.

30 Harold Innis: *Empire and Communications* (Clarendon Press, 1950).

30 "global village": Marshall McLuhan, *The Gutenberg Galaxy* (University of Toronto Press, 1962), 31–2, 219.

30 "ideals and opinions": Royal Commission on Radio Broadcasting, *Report* (King's Printer, 1929), 6.

31 "empty shell": Royal Commission on National Development in the Arts, Letters, and Sciences, *Report* (King's Printer, 1951), 18.

31 "communications are the thread": Royal Commission on Publications, *Report* (Queen's Printer, 1961), 4.

31 "energy in the Executive": *Federalist Papers*, No. 70.

32 Anthony Housefather: "If I were designing a government, I would not combine the executive branch and the legislative branch. I think it makes it very difficult for the legislative branch to exercise its independence. When you have the prime minister and the members of cabinet sitting there and watching what you are saying and doing before you

vote, it is very difficult to exercise proper independence." *Uncommons* podcast, August 2022.

32 fuses executive and legislative powers: Walter Bagehot, *The English Constitution* (H.S. King & Co., 1872), 15–16.

33 "hasty or ill-considered": *Reference re Senate Reform*, 2014 SCC 32.

34 interest groups have more opportunities: Terry Moe and Michael Caldwell, "The Institutional Foundations of Democratic Government: A Comparison of Presidential and Parliamentary Systems," *Journal of Institutional and Theoretical Economics* 150, no. 1 (1994): 171–95; Robert Kagan, *Adversarial Legalism*, 2nd ed. (Harvard University Press, 2019).

34 Restructuring is easier in Canada: Alissa Malkin, "Government Reorganization and the Transfer of Powers," *Ottawa Law Review* 39, no. 3 (2008): 537–70.

34 reorganization within American government: Henry Hogue, *Executive Branch Reorganization* (Washington: Congressional Research Service, 3 August 2017).

35 4,000 appointments: National Task Force on Rule of Law and Democracy, *Proposals for Reform Volume II* (Washington, 2019).

35 Agencies led by appointees: Nick Gallo and David Lewis, "The Consequences of Presidential Patronage for Federal Agency Performance," *Journal of Public Administration Research and Theory* 22, no. 2 (2011): 219–43.

36 "adapt to the changing needs": K.C. Wheare, *Federal Government*, 4th ed. (Oxford University Press, 1968), chapter 11.

36 a distinctive system of federal–provincial diplomacy: Richard Simeon, *Federal-Provincial Diplomacy: The Making of Recent Policy in Canada* (University of Toronto Press, 1973).

37 "governing Canada": John Courtney, "In Defence of Royal Commissions," *Canadian Public Administration* 12, no. 2 (1969): 198–212, 212.

37 "moderation and conciliation": O.D. Skelton, *Life and Letters of Sir Wilfrid Laurier* (Century Co., 1922), 2:380.

37 "exciting subjects": Liberal Party of Canada, *Official Report of the Liberal Convention* (Budget Printing, 1893), 7. In 1849, US president Zachary Taylor also urged fellow politicians to avoid "exciting subjects." See my comments about antebellum American political culture on page 25.

37 "bland works": Jonathan Manthorpe, *The Power and the Tories: Ontario Politics, 1943 to the Present* (Macmillan Canada, 1974).

37 "threads of a thousand acts": *Reference re Secession of Quebec*, [1998] 2 SCR 217.

37 differed substantially from the American approach: Richard Simeon and Beryl Radin, "Reflections on Comparing Federalisms: Canada and the United States," *Publius* 40, no. 3 (2010): 357–65, 359, 361.

40 path to independence: *Reference re Secession of Quebec*; and *Clarity Act*, SC 2000, c. 26.

40 "nation within a nation": CBC *News*, 13 November 2021.

40 "unique culture and shared identity": David Parkinson, "Alberta Will Pay for Playing the Role of Constitutional Problem Child," *Globe and Mail*, 11 December 2022.

41 "Indigenous governance revolution": Douglas Brown, Herman Bakvis, and Gerald Baier, *Contested Federalism: Certainty and Ambiguity in the Canadian Federation*, 2nd ed. (Oxford University Press, 2019), 248.

41 "monitory democracy": John Keane, *The Shortest History of Democracy* (The Experiment, 2022), 131–88.

Chapter Three

46 "Coney Island cowboys": Gerald Clark, "The Many Faces of Pierre Trudeau," *Honolulu Star-Bulletin*, 11 May 1970, C4.

47 "Let the morrow": *Dublin University Magazine* 17, no. 102 (1841): 778.

47 "Democratic myopia": William Nordhaus, "The Political Business Cycle," *Review of Economic Studies* 42 (1975): 169–90.

48 "We are like the pilots": G. Bruce Doern, "Recent Changes in the Philosophy of Policy-Making in Canada," *Canadian Journal of Political Science* 4, no. 2 (1971): 243–64.

48 "constant avalanche": Jerry Grafstein, *A Leader Must Be a Leader: Encounters with Eleven Prime Ministers* (Mosaic Press, 2019), xvii.

48 one of the scarcest resources: Michael Pitfield, "The Shape of Government in the 1980s," *Canadian Public Administration* 19, no. 1 (1976): 8–20, 16.

48 "men and women worn down": J.L. Granatstein, *The Ottawa Men: The Civil Service Mandarins, 1935–1957* (Oxford University Press, 1982), 1.

48 "unbelievable": Liane Benoit, *Ministerial Staff: The Life and Times of Parliament's Statutory Orphans* (Commission of Inquiry into the Sponsorship Program, 2006), 178.

49 "a planet away": Tony Blair, *A Journey: My Political Life* (Alfred A. Knopf, 2010), 20, 132.

49 "organize at a previously unachievable rate": Public Order Emergency Commission, *Report, Volume 1: Overview* (2023), 29.

49 "Voters are promiscuous": *It's Political with Althia Raj* podcast, 5 May 2023.

50 "no fixed electoral cycle": The Harper government adopted legislation in 2007 to establish a fixed four-year election cycle, but for various reasons it is largely ineffectual.

50 "kindergarten children": Paul Wells, "The Elements of Marc Garneau," *Substack*, 15 March 2023.

50 "grinding": Wilson-Raybould, *Indian in the Cabinet: Speaking Truth To Power* (HarperCollins, 2021), 94–102.

51 "a constant struggle": Michael Wernick, *Governing Canada: A Guide to the Tradecraft of Politics* (OnPoint Press, 2021), 108–11.

51 "long work hours": Abbas Rana, "After a 'Disastrous Start' to the Year, Shuffle of Senior PMO and Chiefs of Staff a 'Course Correct in Anticipation of Things to Come,' Say Political Players," *Hill Times*, 13 February 2023.

51 "trying to figure out": Alex Marland, *Brand Command: Canadian Politics and Democracy in the Age of Message Control* (UBC Press, 2016), 383.

51 Steve Outhouse, "It's No Wonder People Burn Out," *On Background* podcast, published by iPolitics, 22 December 2023.

51 "your ability to focus": *CTVNews.ca*, 8 January 2023.

51 "Where do you get the time": podcast, *The Paul Wells Show*, published by *Toronto Star*, 29 March 2023.

52 Parties now behave like contractors: Alex Marland, *Whipped: Party Discipline in Canada* (UBC Press, 2020), 35.

53 "a detailed costed agenda": Eddie Goldenberg, *The Way It Works: Inside Ottawa* (McClelland & Stewart, 2006), 48.

53 Conventional wisdom in the 1970s: Susan Delacourt, *Shopping for Votes*, 2nd ed. (Douglas & McIntyre, 2016), chapter 3.

53 "Issues Change from Year to Year": Stephen Clarkson, *The Big Red Machine: How the Liberal Party Dominates Canadian Politics* (UBC Press, 2005), 39.

53 "detailed, well thought out": Goldenberg, *The Way It Works*, 49, 51.

54 "election platform costing service": *CBC News*, 18 April 2019.

54 "suggesting that there was a strong incentive": Jennifer Robson, "Public Costing of Party Platforms," *Canadian Tax Journal* 68, no. 2 (2020): 505–15, 513.

54 "more important than ever": David Zussman, *Off and Running: The Prospects and Pitfalls of Government Transitions in Canada* (University of Toronto Press, 2013), 93–4, 177–80.

54 50 per cent of its promises: Lisa Birch and François Pétry, *Assessing Justin Trudeau's Liberal Government* (Presses de l'Université Laval, 2019), 15.

55 "the science of delivery": Michael Barber, *How to Run a Government* (Allen Lane, 2015).

55 "pillow forts in the basement": Paul Wells, "This Liberal Resolution Targets My Work," *Substack*, 5 May 2023.

55 drafting the campaign platform: Greg Flynn, "Rethinking Policy Capacity in Canada," *Canadian Public Administration* 54, no. 2 (2011): 235–53, 241–4; William P. Cross, Scott Pruysers, and Rob Currie-Wood, *The Political Party in Canada* (UBC Press, 2022), 183; Bill Morneau, *Where To from Here* (ECW Press, 2023), 253; Delacourt, *Shopping for Votes*; David McGrane, *The New NDP* (UBC Press, 2019); Marland, *Whipped*, chapter 5.

55 "Party leaders appoint platform teams": Yaroslav Baran, "The Political 'Policy' Convention," *Hill Times*, 6 September 2023.

55 focus on the short term: Greg Flynn and Marguerite Marlin, "The Policy Capacity of Political Parties in Canada," in *Policy Analysis in Canada*, eds. Laurent Dobuzinskis and Michael Howlett (Policy Press, 2018), 257–74, 264.

56 "firm and detailed policy decisions": Scott Cameron, "Independent Platform Costing," *Canadian Tax Journal* 68, no. 2 (2020): 491–504, 493.

56 Canadian political parties have little capacity: Marland, *Whipped*, chapter 8; R. Paul Wilson, "The Work of Canadian Political Staffers in Parliamentary Caucus Research Offices," *Canadian Public Administration* 63, no. 3 (2020): 498–521; Jim Miller, "Opposition Research," in *The Palgrave Encyclopedia of Interest Groups, Lobbying and Public Affairs*, eds. Phil Harris, et al. (Springer, 2020), 1–4.

56 A 2021 study: Cross, Pruysers, and Currie-Wood, *The Political Party in Canada*, 182.

56 "are invariably later found": Goldenberg, *The Way It Works*, 47–8.

56 "There are some things": *Boys in Short Pants* podcast, 21 February 2023.

57 "When we have elections": podcast, *The Paul Wells Show*, published by *Toronto Star*, 29 March 2023. For a similar argument, see Eugene Lang, "Ministerial Mandate Letters: Another Nail in the Coffin of Cabinet Government," *Policy Options*, 15 February 2022.

57 Proof Strategies poll: *The Crisis of Trust in Government and Democracy* (Proof Strategies, 2023), 18–19.

58 "the intellectual capacity": Tuna Baskoy, Bryan Evans, and John Shields, "Assessing Policy Capacity in Canada's Public Services: Perspectives of Deputy and Assistant Deputy Ministers," *Canadian Public Administration* 54, no. 2 (2011): 217–34, 231.

58 "central strategic problem": Privy Council Office, *Strengthening Our Policy Capacity* (Privy Council Office, 1996), 6, 20, 38–40.

58 Policy Research Initiative: Herman Bakvis, "Rebuilding Policy Capacity in the Era of the Fiscal Dividend," *Governance* 13, no. 1 (2000): 71–103; Jean-Pierre Voyer, "Policy Analysis in the Federal Government: Building the Forward-Looking Policy Research Capacity," in *Policy Analysis in Canada*, eds. Laurent Dobuzinskis, Michael Howlett, and David Laycock (University of Toronto Press, 2007), 219–37, 224, 235; Leslie Pal, *Beyond Policy Analysis: Public Issue Management in Turbulent Times*, 3rd ed. (Nelson, 2006), 28.

59 A 2015 study of policy capacity: Adam Wellstead, "From Fellegi to Fonberg: Canada's Policy Capacity Groundhog Day?," *Canadian Public Administration* 62, no. 1 (2019): 166–72.

59 "streamlined and less wasteful": Department of Finance, *Budget Speech*, 1992.

59 Some suspected: Laurent Dobuzinskis, "Back to the Future: Is There a Case for Re-Establishing the Economic Council or the Science Council?" (paper, Annual Meeting of the Canadian Political Science Association, Winnipeg, 3 June 2004), 9–10.

59 "blindsiding the Canadian polity": *Ottawa Citizen*, 28 February 1992, A9.

59 "important to the country's prosperity": *Ottawa Citizen*, 27 February 1992, 5.

59 "shooting itself in the head": Jeffrey Kinder and Paul Dufour, *A Lantern on the Bow: A History of the Science Council of Canada* (Invenire, 2018), 289.

59 "like gouging out your eyes": *Calgary Herald*, 26 February 1992, A6.

60 "long gone": Evert Lindquist, "From an Uncomfortable Conversation to a Productive Strategic Dialogue," *Canadian Public Administration* 61, no. 3 (2018): 420–4, 424.

60 "a complete rethink of our system": Morneau, *Where To from Here*, 218–19.

60 reprise of the Macdonald Commission: Richard Nimijean and David Carment, "Rethinking the Canada–US Relationship after the Pandemic," *Policy Options*, 7 May 2020.

60 reprise of the Massey Commission: Senate Prosperity Action Group, *Rising to the Challenge of New Global Realities* (Senate of Canada, 2021).

61 royal commission to draw lessons from the pandemic: *Toronto Globe and Mail*, 19 August 2022.

61 reprise of the Glassco Commission: Kathryn May, "Canada Needs a Royal Commission to Deal with Problems with the Federal Public Service," *Policy Options*, 6 December 2022.

61 royal commission on healthcare: Sergio Marchi, "Canada Needs a Joint Federal-Provincial Commission on Health Care," *Montreal Gazette*, 24 February 2023.

61 "within a four year electoral calendar": Morneau, *Where To from Here*, 218–19.

61 "One of the things that a politician will do": Institute for Public Administration of Canada, "40 Years On: A Yes Minister Tribute," YouTube, 13 November 2020.

62 Morneau later lamented: Morneau, *Where To from Here*, 107–8.

63 Canada has about one hundred think tanks: James McGann, *2020 Global to Go Think Tank Index Report* (University of Pennsylvania, 2021), 44.

63 "connections are more important": Daniel Gold, "Lobbying Regulation in Canada and the United States" (University of Ottawa, 2020), 322.

63 "All think tank leaders": Evert Lindquist, *Think Tanks, Foundations and Policy Discourse* (Canadian Policy Research Networks, 2006), 7.

63 A 2018 study: Donald E. Abelson, *Do Think Tanks Matter? Assessing the Impact of Public Policy Institutes*, 3rd ed. (McGill-Queen's University Press, 2018), table 1.2.

63 More than $20 million: Marsha McLeod, Janice Dickson, and Marieke Walsh, "Convoy Protests Raised $24-million," *Globe and Mail*, 3 November 2022.

63 a budget of only $3 million: Institute for Research on Public Policy, *Annual Report 2021–2022*, 39.

Chapter Four

69 "conduce to the more efficient working": Royal Commission on Dominion-Provincial Relations, *Report* (King's Printer, 1939), 2:70–1.

69 "natural": Darrell Braidwood, "A Survey of Dominion-Provincial Conferences," MA thesis, University of British Columbia, 1941, 1, 4.

69 "built into Canada's constitution": Don McGillivray, "Behind Closed Doors," *Calgary Herald*, 10 December 1965, 4.

70 "real promise": Task Force on Canadian Unity, *A Future Together: Observations and Recommendations* (Minister of Supply and Services Canada, 1979), 74, 99.

70 "to ensure a regular opportunity": Letter from Brian Mulroney to Newfoundland Premier Clyde Wells, 2 November 1989.

70 "the principal forum": Stuart MacKinnon, quoted in Martin Papillon and Richard Simeon, "The Weakest Link? First Ministers' Conferences in Canadian Intergovernmental Relations," in *Canada: The State of the Federation, 2002*, eds. J.P. Meekison, H. Telford, and H. Lazar (Institute of Intergovernmental Relations, 2004), 113–40, 113–14.

70 "to provide essential recognition": Royal Commission on the Economic Union and Development Prospects for Canada, *Report* (Supply and Services Canada, 1985), 3:399.

71 "Prolonged palavers": Jeffrey Simpson, *The Friendly Dictatorship* (McClelland & Stewart, 2001), 85.

71 "through the wringer"; "At the outset of the meeting": Chrétien, *My Years as Prime Minister* (Vintage, 2008), chapter 11.

71 "make-a-deal federalism": Peter Russell, *Constitutional Odyssey: Can Canadians Become a Sovereign People?*, 3rd ed. (University of Toronto Press, 2004), 186.

72 "a core institutional feature"/"ad hoc and sporadic": Papillon and Simeon, "The Weakest Link," 121.

72 "strengthen intergovernmental cooperation": Conservative Party of Canada, *Stand Up for Canada* (2006), 43.

72 "Alex could just barely contain himself": Paul Wells, *The Longer I'm Prime Minister: Stephen Harper and Canada* (Vintage Canada, 2014), 83.

72 "The grand gesture": John Ibbitson, *Stephen Harper* (Signal, 2015), 268.

73 "a very preliminary discussion": David Akin and Andrew Mayeda, "Harper, Premiers on Same Page on Investment Spending," *National Post*, 11 November 2008, 5.

73 "called at the whim": Gregory J. Inwood, Patricia L. O'Reilly, and Carolyn M. Johns, *Intergovernmental Policy Capacity in Canada* (McGill-Queen's University Press, 2011), 86.

73 "Bilateralism": Christopher Dunn, "Harper without Jeers, Trudeau without Cheers," *IRPP Insight*, no. 8 (2016), 8.

73 "something it hadn't experienced": Ibbitson, *Stephen Harper*, 271.

73 "His eschewing of First Ministers' Meetings": Jennifer Ditchburn and Graham Fox, *The Harper Factor: Assessing a Prime Minister's Policy Legacy* (McGill-Queen's University Press, 2016), 7–8.

73 "every single year": Mark Kennedy, "Trudeau Pledges Annual Meeting with Premiers If He Wins Election," *Ottawa Citizen*, 20 December 2014.

74 "run into the temptation": Wernick, *Governing Canada*, 63–5.

74 "urgent call": Council of the Federation, "Canada's Premiers Looking to Partner with Federal Government on Health Care Sustainability," News release, 12 July 2022.

74 "came fast and furious": Ian Bailey, "Ottawa Offers Premiers $46.2-billion in New Health Care Funding," *Globe and Mail*, 7 February 2023.

75 "an important opportunity": Office of the Premier, Government of the Yukon, "Western Premiers Conclude Meetings in Regina," 27 May 2022.

75 "to promote unity of purpose": Donald J. Savoie, *Federal-Provincial Collaboration* (McGill-Queen's University Press, 1981), 21.

75 "a significant intergovernmental institution": David Cameron and Richard Simeon, "Intergovernmental Relations in Canada: The Emergence of Collaborative Federalism," *Publius* 32, no. 2 (2002): 49–71, 61.

76 "one, single, united voice": Trevor Wright, "Canadian Premiers Call for First Ministers Meeting on Healthcare in New Year," *Nunavut News*, 9 December 2022.

77 "like-minded countries": Barack Obama, quoted by Radio France Internationale, 26 May 2016. https://www.rfi.fr/en/economy/20160526-g7-better-without-russia.

77 "govern together": John Kirton, "Governing Together: The Gx Future," *Studia Diplomatica* 68, no. 3 (2017): 7–28.

77 "discuss major, often complex international issues": G7 Information Centre, "What Are the G7 and G8?," http://www.g7.utoronto.ca/what_is_g8.html.

77 "pretty essential": *CTV News*, 26 June 2010.

77 "an important opportunity": Giuseppe Valiante, "Trudeau Defends $600-million Cost of Quebec G7 Summit," *Toronto Star*, 24 May 2018.

77 "frank and open discussion": Government of Canada, "Canada and the G7," September 2023, https://www.international.gc.ca/world-monde/international_relations-relations_internationales/g7/index.aspx.

78 "cooperation in the national interest": Kenneth Wiltshire, "Australia's New Federalism: Recipes for Marble Cakes," *Publius* 22, no. 3 (1992): 165–80, 175.

78 "shared vision": K.D. Saksena, *NITI Aayog and Planning Commission* (Shipra Publications, 2019), 6.

79 "increasingly obvious": Jonathan Olsen, *The European Union: Politics and Policies*, 7th ed. (Routledge, 2021), 106.

79 "general political directions": Treaty on European Union, Article 15.

79 "political power station": Luuk van Middelaar, *Alarums & Excursions: Improvising Politics on the European Stage* (Agenda Publishing, 2019), 270.

80 "full adult suffrage": R.M. Dawson, *The Government of Canada* (University of Toronto Press, 1949), 380.

80 "unfettered by Indian treaties": R.M. Dawson and Norman Ward, *The Government of Canada*, 5th ed. (University of Toronto Press, 1970), 64.

80 "limited and minimal promises": Government of Canada, *Statement on Indian Policy* (Department of Indian Affairs and Northern Development, 1969), 11.

81 "third order": Royal Commission on Aboriginal Peoples, *Report* (1996).

81 a composite of two federations: Frances Abele and Michael J. Prince, "Four Pathways to Aboriginal Self-Government in Canada," *American Review of Canadian Studies* 36, no. 4 (2006): 568–95, 579.

81 "multi-level governance": Christopher Alcantara and Jen Nelles, "Indigenous Peoples and the State in Settler Societies: Toward a More Robust Definition of Multilevel Governance," *Publius* 44, no. 1 (2014): 183–204.

81 “full partners”: Truth and Reconciliation Commission of Canada, *Final Report, Volume One* (Toronto: James Lorimer & Company Ltd., Publishers, 2015), 326.

81 “indirectly as supplicants”: Gurston Dacks, “The Social Union Framework Agreement and the Role of Aboriginal Peoples in Canadian Federalism,” *American Review of Canadian Studies* 31, no. 1–2 (2001): 301–15, 306.

81 “automatic inclusion”: Alcantara and Nelles, “Indigenous Peoples and the State,” 194.

82 “shrugged off the request”: Rosemary Speirs, “Stewart Needs PM in Her Corner,” *Saskatoon Star-Phoenix*, 1 April 1999, 4.

82 “excluded … from any meaningful role”; ”depends on whether”: Alcantara and Nelles, “Indigenous Peoples and the State,” 194, 198.

82 “wait outside of rooms”: *CBC News*, 7 February 2023.

82 “partners of the federation”: Council of the Federation Founding Agreement, 5 December 2003, 1.

83 “at the choice of premiers”: Jared Wesley, “National Indigenous Groups and the Premiers’ Meeting,” *Policy Options*, 16 August 2017.

83 “just another special interest group”: “AFN Accuses Some Provincial and Territorial Leaders of ‘Regressive Moves’ to Minimize and Marginalize Indigenous Leaders,” *Windspeaker.com*, 17 July 2017.

83 “still not full-fledged partners”: Martin Papillon, “Nation to Nation? Canadian Federalism and Indigenous Multi-Level Governance,” in *Canadian Federalism*, eds. Herman Bakvis and Grace Skogstad (University of Toronto Press, 2020), 395–426, 414.

Chapter Five

87 In the 1980s, the newspaper industry: Frederick Fletcher et al., *The Newspaper and Public Affairs* (Royal Commission on Newspapers, 1981); Don Munton, “Public Opinion and the Media in Canada from Cold War to Détente to New Cold War,” *International Journal* 39, no. 1 (1983): 171–213, 199–202; Frederick J. Fletcher, “Mass Media and Parliamentary Elections in Canada,” *Legislative Studies Quarterly* 12, no. 3 (1987): 341–72, 351.

88 People engaged in other ways too: Rick Van Loon, “Political Participation in Canada: The 1965 Election,” *Canadian Journal*

of Political Science 3, no. 3 (1970): 376–99; Carole Uhlaner, "The Consistency of Individual Political Participation across Governmental Levels in Canada," *American Journal of Political Science* 26, no. 2 (1982): 298–311.

88 Today, news is consumed in radically different ways: Reuters Institute, *Digital News Report 2022* (Reuters Institute for the Study of Journalism, 2022), 10–11, 43, 119; Sam Andrey et al., *Rebuilding Canada's Public Square* (Ryerson Leadership Lab, 2021), 8–9; Online Business Canada, "Social Media Use in Canada, 2022," https://canadiansinternet.com/2022-report-social-media-use-in-canada-statistics/; David Akin, "PCO Poll Finds Many Do Not Trust the Media," *Global News*, 27 December 2023.

89 "set the rules for public deliberation": Jamie Susskind, *The Digital Republic* (Pegasus Books, 2022), 267–8.

89 trust in the public broadcaster: Reuters Institute, *Digital News Report 2022*, 17.

90 five were American-owned: Future of Media Project, https://projects.iq.harvard.edu/futureofmedia/canadian-media-ownership.

90 In a 2022 survey: Reuters Institute, *Digital News Report 2022*, 119.

90 disinformation campaigns: Stephanie Carvin, *Stand on Guard: Reassessing Threats to Canada's National Security* (University of Toronto Press, 2021), chapter 7.

91 "more rapid exhaustion": Philipp Lorenz-Spreen et al., "Accelerating Dynamics of Collective Attention," *Nature Communications* 10, no. 1 (2019): 1759. The problem of information overload and exhaustion is also examined by psychologist Gloria Marks in *Attention Span* (Hanover Square Press, 2023).

91 "Some days it feels like": Ronald Deibert, *Reset: Reclaiming the Internet for Civil Society* (House of Anansi, 2020), 300.

91 A 2022 cross-national study: Reuters Institute, *Digital News Report 2022*, 10, 12–14.

91 A 2023 US survey: Pew Research Center, "Americans Are Following the News Less Closely than They Used To," 24 October 2023.

92 a new epoch of democracy: Lawrence K. Grossman, *The Electronic Republic: Reshaping Democracy in the Information Age* (Viking, 1995).

92 "civilization of the mind": James Perry Barlow, "A Declaration of the Independence of Cyberspace," 8 February 1996.

92 "feelings of distress": UNDP, *Human Development Report 2021/2022*, 9–10.

92 2021 Statistics Canada study: Statistics Canada, "Perceived Life Stress, by Age Group," https://www150.statcan.gc.ca/t1/tbl1/en/tv.action?pid=1310009604.

92 40 per cent of Canadian workers: Linda Duxbury and Christopher Higgins, *Revisiting Work-Life Issues in Canada: The 2012 National Study on Balancing Work and Caregiving in Canada* (Carleton University, 2012), 7.

92 2022 Freedom Convoy inquiry: Public Order Emergency Commission, *Report, Volume 2: Analysis* (2023), 75–7.

92 almost two hours a day: Online Business Canada, "Social Media Use in Canada, 2022," https://canadiansinternet.com/2022-report-social-media-use-in-canada-statistics/. The effects of social media use that are described in this paragraph are affirmed in a recent report from the Surgeon General of the United States: *Social Media and Youth Mental Health* (May 2023).

92 "attention engineering": Johann Hari, *Stolen Focus: Why You Can't Pay Attention and How to Think Deeply Again* (Crown, 2022).

92 "compulsive, prolonged, and unhealthy use": Complaint for injunctive and other relief, *State of Arizona et al. v. Meta Platforms et al.*, United States District Court for the Northern District of California, 24 October 2023.

93 separation anxiety: Michelle Cleary, Sancia West, and Denis Visentin, "The Mental Health Impacts of Smartphone and Social Media Use," *Issues in Mental Health Nursing* 41, no. 8 (2020): 755–7.

93 2018 Statistics Canada survey: Christoph Schimmele, Jonathan Fonberg, and Grant Schellenberg, "Canadians' Assessment of Social Media in Their Lives," *Statistics Canada Economic and Social Reports* 1, no. 3 (2021).

93 "strengthen our social fabric": Julia Carrie Wong, "How Facebook Groups Bring People Closer Together," *The Guardian*, 31 July 2017.

93 "internet runs on love": Clay Shirky, *Here Comes Everybody* (Penguin, 2009).

93 "the digital age of instant communication": David Johnston, *Trust: Twenty Ways to Build a Better Country* (Penguin Random House, 2022), x.

93 In a 2021 survey: Andrey et al., *Rebuilding Canada's Public Square*, 10.

93 A study of tweets: Samara Centre for Democracy, SAMbot 2021 Federal Election Snapshot, August 2022.

93 Female politicians are disproportionately targeted: Ludovic Rheault, Erica Rayment, and Andreea Musulan, "Politicians in the Line of Fire: Incivility and the Treatment of Women on Social Media," *Research & Politics* 6, no. 1 (2019) 1–7.

93 "I have received non-stop abuse": Christopher Guly, "Twitter Has 'the Most Violent, Misogynistic, Appalling, Anonymous, Horrific Messages,' says Green Party Leader May," *Hill Times*, 1 May 2023.

94 "abusive, misogynistic, and racist engagement": *CTV News*, 12 March 2023.

94 technology-driven disinformation campaigns: Maria Ressa, *How to Stand Up to a Dictator* (HarperCollins, 2022).

94 In a 2023 Statistics Canada survey: Statistics Canada, "Concerns with Mis-information Online," 20 December 2023, https://www150.statcan.gc.ca/n1/daily-quotidien/231220/dq231220b-eng.htm.

94 "digital tribe": Byung-Chul Han, *Infocracy: Digitization and the Crisis of Democracy* (Polity Press, 2022).

94 2022 Abacus survey: Abacus Data, "Millions Believe in Conspiracy Theories in Canada," 12 June 2022, https://abacusdata.ca/conspiracy-theories-canada/.

94 "an accelerant for misinformation": Public Order Emergency Commission, *Report, Volume 1: Analysis*, 29, 141, 265.

95 "the core of the party organization": Royal Commission on Electoral Reform and Party Financing, *Final Report* (Canada Communication Group, 1991), 292.

95 the era of yellow journalism: Minko Sotiron, *From Politics to Profit: The Commercialization of Canadian Daily Newspapers, 1890–1920* (McGill-Queen's University Press, 1997), 18–20.

95 "bettering democracy": Caitlin Cieslik-Miskimen, "Accuracy Always: Willard Bleyer and the Push for Better Journalism," in *Education for Democracy*, ed. Chad Alan Goldberg (University of Wisconsin Press, 2020), 76–96, 85.

95 "The present crisis of Western democracy": Walter Lippmann, *Liberty and the News* (Harcourt, Brace and Howe, 1920), 5.

95 Earnings of Canadian newspapers: Statistics Canada data, Table: 21-10-0191-01.

96 Digital advertising revenues: IAB Canada Internet Advertising Revenue Reports, https://iabcanada.com/research/internet-ad-revenue-reports/.

96 working journalists: Nordicity, *Digital Media at the Crossroads: Measuring the Revenues, the Audiences, and the Future Prospects* (Nordicity, 2020), 15.

96 freelancers, rather than full-time employees: Sabrina Wilkinson, "Canadian Journalism in Decline," *The Conversation*, 19 November 2019.

96 parliamentary press gallery: Beatrice Britneff, "Parliamentary Press Gallery Now the Smallest It's Been in 22 Years," *iPolitics*, 8 December 2016.

96 Canadian Press itself cut staff: Tamara A. Small and Harold J. Jansen, *Digital Politics in Canada: Promises and Realities* (University of Toronto Press, 2020), 160–1.

96 In Ontario, for example: Tamara Small, "Media in Ontario Politics: The Press Gallery in the Twenty-First Century," in *The Politics of Ontario*, eds. Cheryl N. Collier and Jonathan Malloy (University of Toronto Press, 2017), 157–91, 163.

96 300 community newspapers: Public Policy Forum, *The Shattered Mirror Revisited* (2022).

97 2018 study by the Public Policy Forum: Public Policy Forum, *Mind the Gaps: Quantifying the Decline of News Coverage in Canada* (2018), 1.

97 "proliferation of superficial journalism": April Lindgren, "What the Death of Local News Means for the Federal Election," *The Walrus*, 24 April 2019.

97 "withering of a sense of community": Michael Bliss, "Privatizing the Mind: The Sundering of Canadian History," *Journal of Canadian Studies* 26, no. 4 (1992): 5–17, 5.

97 "a nation without memory": J.L. Granatstein, *Who Killed Canadian History?* (HarperCollins, 1998), xviii.

97 "do not know": Desmond Morton, "History-Teaching in Canada," *Policy Options*, 1 November 2002.

98 2006 survey: Henry Milner, *The Internet Generation: Engaged Citizens or Political Dropouts* (University Press of New England, 2010), table 5.1.

98 2023 survey: Pollara, "Canadians Rank the Greatest Prime Minister in Canadian History," January 2023, https://www.pollara.com/canadians-rank-the-greatest-prime-minister-in-canadian-history/.

98 2007 Dominion Institute survey: Caroline Alphonso, "Canadians Don't Know Their Own History, Study Shows," *Globe and Mail*, 9 November 2007.

98 Canadian prime minister is directly elected: Ipsos, "New Survey Demonstrates that Canadians Lack Basic Understanding of Our Parliamentary System," 15 December 2008, https://www.ipsos.com/en-ca/wake-constitutional-crisis-new-survey-demonstrates-canadians-lack-basic-understanding-our-countrys.

98 longest-serving Canadian prime minister: Ipsos Reid, "News Release: O Canada: Our Home and Naïve Land," (Toronto), 1 July 2008.

98 only one in twenty Quebecers: Coalition for History, "The First Prime Minister of Quebec: An Illustrious Unknown," 1 March 2011, https://coalitionhistoire.org/presse/sondage-coalition-pour-lhistoireleger-marketing-le-premier-premier-ministre-du-quebec-un.

98 2022 surveys conducted for the Association for Canadian Studies: Association for Canadian Studies, "Knowledge and Interest in Indigenous peoples in Canada," September 2022; "Examining Canadians' Knowledge of World War I and II," November 2022.

99 "people made important survival decisions": Michael Marker, "Teaching History from an Indigenous Perspective," in *New Possibilities for the Past: Shaping History Education in Canada*, ed. Penney Clark (UBC Press, 2011), 97–112, 98.

99 "[We examine] past events": Niccolò Machiavelli, *Discourses on Livy* (Oxford University Press, 2008), 105.

99 "we are in the stream of history": Ken Osborne, "'To the Past': Why We Need to Teach and Study History," in *To the Past: History Education, Public Memory, and Citizenship in Canada*, ed. R.W. Sandwell (University of Toronto Press, 2006), 107.

99 "Canadians' general ignorance": Patrick Malcolmson et al., *The Canadian Regime: An Introduction to Parliamentary Government in Canada*, 7th ed. (University of Toronto Press, 2021), xii.

100 "I am more convinced than ever": Twitter, @MercedesGlobal, 3 November 2022.

100 A 2021 cross-country study: Historica Canada, *Canadian History Report Card* (2021).

100 Only four of thirteen provinces; "yawning absence": Trilby Kent, *The Vanishing Past* (Sutherland House, 2022), 97, 112.

100 "dabbler": Andrew S. Hughes, Murray Print, and Alan Sears, "Curriculum Capacity and Citizenship Education: A Comparative Analysis of Four Democracies," *Compare* 40, no. 3 (2010): 293–309, 294, 299.

100 "missed opportunities": Email correspondence with author, 24 January 2023.

101 the federal role in civic education: Immigration Refugees and Citizenship Canada, *Evaluation of the Citizenship Program* (2020), 11.

101 2007 survey: Ipsos Reid/Dominion Institute, National Citizenship Exam Ten Year Benchmark Study, 29 June 2007, https://www.ipsos.com/en-ca/dominion-institute-national-citizenship-exam-survey-2007.

101 As the Lortie Commission observed: Royal Commission on Electoral Reform and Party Financing, *Final Report*, 291.

101 "civic journalism for underserved communities": Heritage Canada, "Local Journalism Initiative," https://www.canada.ca/en/canadian-heritage/services/funding/local-journalism-initiative.html.

102 "six-alarm fire": Gregory Taylor and Brooks DeCilla, "Canada: A Strong Foundation with an Uncertain Future," in *The Media for Democracy Monitor 2021*, eds. J. Trappel and T. Tomaz (University of Gothenburg, 2021), 43–84, 46.

102 $300 million in revenue: Parliamentary Budget Office, *Cost Estimate for Bill C-18: Online News Act* (2022), 8.

102 "defund the CBC"; "shut down": @PierrePoilievre, Twitter, 16 April 2023; Proceedings of the Standing Committee on Finance, 29 April 2019.

102 "a woke agency": *Hansard*, 30 March 2023.

102 "back in control": @PierrePoilievre, Twitter, 18 June 2022.

103 "juvenile": Andrew MacDougall, "CBC Debate Highlights the Challenge of Ensuring a Common Understanding," *Ottawa Citizen*, 20 April 2023.

103 "We are standing up": *Hansard*, 20 June 2023.

103 "This is a dispute over democracy": CPAC, 5 July 2023.

103 Liberal Party platforms: These are archived by Poltext, a project of the Centre for Public Policy Analysis at the Université Laval:

https://www.poltext.org/en/part-1-electronic-political-texts/electronic-manifestos-canada.

104 mandate letters: These are published by the Office of the Prime Minister: https://www.pm.gc.ca/en/mandate-letters.

104 "Our mission": Canadian Heritage, *Departmental Performance Report 2014–2015*.

104 "core responsibilities": Department of Canadian Heritage, *Departmental Results Framework, 2023–24*.

105 "ordinary working people": David Ljunggren, "PM Raps 'Out of Touch' Artists Over Cuts," *Reuters*, 23 September 2008.

Chapter Six

107 In the middle of the twentieth century: Robert Presthus, *Elite Accommodation in Canadian Politics* (Macmillan, 1973), chapter 8; John Porter, *The Vertical Mosaic* (University of Toronto Press, 2015), chapters 14 and 17.

108 "slavish adherence": Special Committee on the Review of Personnel Management and the Merit Principle, *Report* (Ottawa, 1979), 5, 52.

108 "The huge bureaucracy": J.L. Granatstein, *The Ottawa Men: The Civil Service Mandarins, 1935–1957* (Oxford University Press, 1982), 279–80.

108 "cautious, uncertain institution": Donald J. Savoie, *Democracy in Canada: The Disintegration of Our Institutions* (McGill-Queen's University Press, 2019), chapter 13.

108 "culture of control and risk avoidance": Kathryn May, "All-Powerful PMO, Mistrust Destroying the Public Service: Tellier," *Policy Options*, May 2022.

108 "an operating culture": Kevin Lynch and Jim Mitchell, "Instead of Adding New Programs, Ottawa Should Focus on Proper Delivery of the Ones It Has," *Globe and Mail*, 11 February 2023.

108 "a core feature": Institute on Governance, *Top of Mind: Answering the Call, Adapting to Change* (Institute on Governance, 2022), 73.

109 public service seems to snap back: Clerk of the Privy Council, *28th Annual Report on the Public Service of Canada* (Privy Council Office, 2021), 18.

110 "web of rules": Advisory Committee on the Public Service, *Third Report to the Prime Minister* (Office of the Prime Minister, 2009).

110 "sets forth the sins": Walter Stewart, "The Man Who Keeps the Government Honest," *Canadian Weekly*, 26 December 1964, 2.

110 "vast expansion": Clinton Free, Vaughan S. Radcliffe, and Brent White, "Crisis, Committees and Consultants: The Rise of Value-for-Money Auditing in the Federal Public Sector in Canada," *Journal of Business Ethics* 113, no. 3 (2013): 441–59, 446.

111 "a government in exile": S.L. Sutherland, *The Office of the Auditor General of Canada: Government in Exile?* (Queen's University School of Policy Studies, 2002).

111 "combative" style: Catherine Liston-Heyes and Luc Juillet, "Institutional Embeddedness and the Language of Accountability: Evidence from 20 Years of Canadian Public Audit Reports," *Financial Accountability & Management* 38, no. 4 (2022): 608–32, 612, 622.

111 Its authority grew immensely in 1918: Alasdair Roberts, *So-Called Experts: How American Consultants Remade the Canadian Civil Service, 1918–1921* (Institute of Public Administration of Canada, 1996).

111 "shaming and blaming": Kathryn May, "Barrados Prepared to Back Up Tough Talk," *Regina Leader-Post*, 24 November 2003, 16.

111 "complex and time-consuming": David Johnson, *Thinking Government: Public Administration and Politics in Canada*, 4th ed. (University of Toronto Press, 2017), 285.

113 "The Taj Mahal of unintended consequences": Antonin Scalia, "The Freedom of Information Act Has No Clothes," *Regulation* 6, no. 2 (1982): 14–20.

113 2000 study: Treasury Board Secretariat, *Review of the Costs Associated with Administering Access to Information and Privacy Legislation*, 2000.

113 another study twenty years later: Treasury Board Secretariat, *Costing Study of the Access to Information Regime*, 2022.

113 "the same blaze of publicity": *House of Commons Debates*, 18 September 1995.

113 "biggest scandal": Jack Aubry, "Biggest Scandal in Canadian History," *Ottawa Citizen*, 28 January 2000.

114 "an environment that emphasized service": Denis Saint-Martin, "Managerialist Advocate or 'Control Freak'? The Janus-Faced Office of the Auditor General," *Canadian Public Administration* 47, no. 2 (2004): 121–40, 132.

114 "one of the most extensive": David A. Good, *The Politics of Public Management: The HRDC Audit of Grants and Contributions* (University of Toronto Press, 2003), 7, 127.

114 $50 million annually: S.L. Sutherland, "'Biggest Scandal in Canadian History'": HRDC Audit Starts Probity War," *Critical Perspectives on Accounting* 14, no. 1 (2003): 187–224, 214.

114 The inquiry itself cost $70 million: "Cleaning Up Sponsorship Mess May Cost $80-Million," *Globe and Mail*, 20 February 2005.

114 "The vast majority": Commission of Inquiry into the Sponsorship Program, *Who Is Responsible? Fact Finding Report* (2005), xx–xxi.

114 "Gomery effect": David Zussman, "The Precarious State of the Public Service," in *How Ottawa Spends 2010–2011*, eds. Bruce Doern and Christopher Stoney (McGill-Queen's University Press, 2010), 219–42.

115 "a growing preoccupation": Catherine Liston-Heyes and Luc Juillet, "What Has Become of the Audit Explosion? Analyzing Trends in Oversight Activities in the Canadian Government," *Public Administration* 100, no. 4 (2022): 1073–90, 1074.

118 "monitory democracy": John Keane, *The Shortest History of Democracy* (The Experiment, 2022), 150.

118 important innovation in democratic rule: S.L. Sutherland and G. Bruce Doern, *Bureaucracy in Canada: Control and Reform, Collected Research Studies* (University of Toronto Press, 1985).

118 "never happens again": The phrase used by HRDC minister Jane Stewart in 2000 and Stephen Harper in 2005.

118 "I have become increasingly troubled": Auditor General of Canada, *Annual Report for the Fiscal Year Ended March 31, 1987*.

119 A 2015 report from the Public Policy Forum: *Time for a Reboot* (2015), 6–7.

119 about 600 political staff: Jonathan Craft estimates that there were 560 exempt staff in 2014: *Backrooms and Beyond: Partisan Advisers and the Politics of Policy Work in Canada* (University of Toronto Press, 2016), appendix A. The number has likely grown over the past decade. More than 700 individuals are listed in a 2023 directory of ministerial staff: *Inside Ottawa: Ministers' Offices Fall 2023* (Hill Times, 2023).

120 "barely knew the names": See Ritchie's comments on Michael Wernick's *Governing Canada*, on https://www.amazon.ca/product-reviews/0774890533.

120 "treated like race horses": Fred Delorey, *On Background* podcast, published by iPolitics, 22 December 2023.

120 "countervailing" force: Liane Benoit, *Ministerial Staff: The Life and Times of Parliament's Statutory Orphans* (Commission of Inquiry into the Sponsorship Program, 2006), 161.

120 "challenge function": R. Paul Wilson, "Trust but Verify: Ministerial Policy Advisors and Public Servants in the Government of Canada," *Canadian Public Administration* 59, no. 3 (2016): 337–56, 339.

121 "young, ambitious, and politically loyal": Benoit, *Ministerial Staff*, 146.

121 "ministerial staffers are not as experienced": Jennifer Robson and R. Paul Wilson, "Political Staff and Permanent Public Servants: Still Not Getting Along," in *Political Elites in Canada*, eds. Alex Marland, Thierry Giasson, and Andrea Lawlor (UBC Press, 2018), 71–88, 83.

121 "pumped with adrenalin": Wernick, *Governing Canada*, 44.

121 "seized by a rapid response mentality": Alex Marland, *Whipped: Party Discipline in Canada* (UBC Press, 2020), 169.

121 "did not hesitate to drive": Ian Brodie, *At the Centre of Government* (McGill-Queen's University Press, 2018), 121.

121 "intrusive, obstructive": Jacques Bourgault and James Iain Gow, "Canada's Top Public Servants Meet Agency Theory in the Harper Years," *International Review of Administrative Sciences* 88, no. 2 (2022): 302–19, 309.

121 "I have middle managers": Privy Council Office, *Report of the Deputy Ministers' Task Team on Values and Ethics*, December 2023, https://www.canada.ca/en/privy-council/services/publications/deputy-ministers-task-team-values-ethics-report-clerk-privy-council.html.

122 "There's a short-termism": Robson and Wilson, "Political Staff and Permanent Public Servants," 78.

122 "the over-responsiveness of public servants": Public Service Commission, *Merit and Non-Partisanship under the Public Service Employment Act* (2011), 18.

122 Senior officials are more hesitant: Ralph Heintzman, *Renewal of the Federal Public Service: Toward a Charter of Public Service* (Canada 2020, 2014), 19–20; Donald J. Savoie, "Searching for Accountability in a Government without Boundaries," *Canadian Public Administration* 47, no. 1 (2004): 1–26; Institute on Governance, *Top of Mind*.

122 "no surprises environment": Craft, *Backrooms and Beyond*, 24.

122 "There's a huge amount of self-policing": Alex Marland, *Brand Command: Canadian Politics and Democracy in the Age of Message Control*, (UBC Press, 2016), 281.

124 "fewer conventional opportunities": Privy Council Office, *Report of the Deputy Ministers' Task Team on Values and Ethics.*

124 The service has grown: Data on the size of the federal public service is published by Treasury Board Secretariat at https://www.canada.ca/en/treasury-board-secretariat/services/innovation/human-resources-statistics/population-federal-public-service.html.

124 "grand inquest": J.E. Hodgetts, "The Grand Inquest on the Canadian Public Service." *Australian Journal of Public Administration* 22, no. 3 (1963): 226–41.

124 "systemic flexibility"; "revolutionary milestone": Michel D'Avignon, "The Royal Commission on Government Organization: A Study in Bureaucracy and Innovation," MA thesis, Carleton University, 1972.

125 "a broad conversation": Email from John Hannaford to deputy ministers, 18 September 2023.

Chapter Seven

129 "the absence of a big-ideas, priorities agenda": Mel Cappe, *The Tansley Lecture: Analysis and Evidence for Good Public Policy* (Johnson Shoyama Graduate School of Public Policy, 2011).

131 "an early warning and reconnaissance system": Friedrich Ebert Stiftung, *Annual Report 2021* (August 2022), 40.

131 "vitalize and stabilize": Hartwig Pautz, "Think-Tanks in Germany: The Bertelsmann Foundation's Role in Labour Market Reform," *Zeitschrift für Politikberatung* 1, no. 3/4 (2008): 437–56, 439.

131 The idea of establishing party foundations: Royal Commission on Electoral Reform and Party Financing, *Final Report*, 290–302. A similar proposal was made by New Brunswick's Commission on Legislative Democracy: *Final Report* (2004), 23–4.

132 disagreements can have fatal consequences: Jocalyn Clark, Sharon Straus, Adam Houston, and Kamran Abbasi, "The World Expected More of Canada," *BMJ* 382 (2023): 1634.

133 "routinized federal-provincial summitry": J.S. Dupré, "Reflections on the Workability of Executive Federalism," in *Perspectives on Canadian*

Federalism, ed. R. Olling and M. Westmacott (Prentice-Hall, 1988), 250–1.

133 Richard Simeon and Martin Papillon suggested in 2004: Martin Papillon and Richard Simeon, "The Weakest Link? First Ministers' Conferences in Canadian Intergovernmental Relations," in *Canada: The State of the Federation, 2002*, eds. J.P. Meekison, H. Telford, and H. Lazar (Institute of Intergovernmental Relations, 2004), 130–1.

133 "trust ties": Hamish Telford, "The Spending Power Revisited," *IRPP Policy Matters* 9, no. 3, 12–53, 41.

135 "informed democratic discourse": Public Policy Forum, *Mind the Gaps*, 1.

135 "Canadian public conversation": Mike Harris and Preston Manning, *Vision for a Canada Strong and Free* (Fraser Institute, 2007), 206.

135 "give Canadians back control of their lives": @PierrePoilievre, Twitter, 9 April 2022.

136 "The need has never been greater": Jeffrey Kinder and Paul Dufour, *A Lantern on the Bow: A History of the Science Council of Canada* (Invenire, 2018), 15. See also Laurent Dobuzinskis, "Back to the Future: Is There a Case for Re-Establishing the Economic Council or the Science Council?" (paper, Annual Meeting of the Canadian Political Science Association, Winnipeg, 3 June 2004).

137 "national regulatory systems require periodic maintenance": OECD, *Good Governance and Regulatory Management* (2001), 5.

137 "nobody knows what to do about it": Quoted in Kathryn May, "Canada Needs a Royal Commission to Deal with Problems with the Federal Public Service," *Policy Options*, 6 December 2022.

138 "Canada has allowed its supply chain": *Globe and Mail*, 11 February 2023.

138 "rethink of the direction": Daniel Caron, Evert Lindquist, and Robert Shepherd, "Critical Considerations for the Future of the Public Service," *Policy Options*, 14 February 2023.

140 "democratic recession": Larry Diamond, "Facing Up to the Democratic Recession," *Journal of Democracy* 26, no. 1 (January 2015): 141–55.

140 "forward-looking": Address to a study session at the Party School of the CPC Central Committee, 6 February 2023.

Index

The letter *f* following a page number denotes a figure.

About the Author

Alasdair Roberts is professor of public policy at the University of Massachusetts Amherst. He was born in Temiskaming Shores, Ontario. He received his BA from Queen's University, his JD from the University of Toronto, and his PhD from Harvard University. In 2007, Professor Roberts was elected as a fellow of the US National Academy of Public Administration. In 2022, he received the Riggs Award for Lifetime Achievement in International and Comparative Administration from the American Society for Public Administration. In 2022–23, he was the Jocelyne Bourgon Visiting Scholar at the Canada School of Public Service. He has written ten previous books.

